Jodie Sewall

The Blessing

Experiencing Renewal in Valley Places

Happy are the people whose strength is in You; whose hearts are set on pilgrimage. As they pass through the Valley of Tears, they make it a source of springwater; even the autumn rain will cover it with blessings. They go from strength to strength; each appears before God in Zion. Psalm 84:5-7

I am so thankful that Jesus showed Himself faithful to a dear sister in Christ through her painful valley walk. I am thankful that even when she felt like she didn't have the strength to go on and had pretty much given up on Jesus that did not give up on her. I am ever so thankful that God strengthened her each day and that He gently led her out of the Valley of Tears having accomplished a marvelous work of faith in her life and in mine and others who prayed for her. It was because of her great trial and a smaller one of my own that I sat down to study this Valley of Tears and in this study I found <u>The Blessing</u>!

Thank you to my dear sweet friends at Word of Life who let me brainstorm my ideas and lessons and offer me their feedback and their encouragement.

Truly God has blessed us all and because of all my friends I feel most blessed of all!!

The Blessing
Experiencing Renewal in Valley Places
2013, Revised 2018

Sewall Publishing

ISBN: 978-0-578-12972-3

All Rights Reserved
Printed in the United States of America

Cover Photos: Shutterstock- Standard License; Image #106330676 copyright Andre1UC88 Image #118325788 copyright biletskiy

Unless otherwise noted, all Scripture quotations are taken from the Holman Christian Standard Bible® Copyright © 1999, 2000, 2002, 2003 by Holman Bible Publishers. Used by permission. Holman Christian Standard Bible®, Holman CSB®, and HCSB® are federally registered trademarks of Holman Bible Publishers.

THE HOLY BIBLE, NEW INTERNATIONAL VERSION®, NIV® Copyright © 1973, 1978, 1984, 2011 by Biblica, Inc.™ Used by permission. All rights reserved worldwide.

TABLE OF CONTENTS

Know what you Believe 5

- He Does Not Change 11
- He Is My Father 13
- He Loves Me 16
- He Is With Me 18
- He Brings Peace 20

The Refining Valley of Transformation – Because He promised 24

- God's Vision for Us 30
- The Favored One 32
- A Meek Spirit 35
- The Giver or the Gift 38
- Highly Esteemed 42

The Valley of Correction – Because He Loves Me 46

- He Speaks to Me, Am I Listening? 51
- Generational Thinking 53
- Against Thee and Thee Only 56
- Muttering Against God 58
- Common or Holy? 59

The Valley of His Presence – That I Might Know Him 63

- When Did They Know Him? 67
- He Brought Peace 68
- Who by Faith 70
- The World Was Not Worthy of Them! 72
- Rumors or Vision? 73

The Valley of Glory – That Others May See Him in Me 75

- This Mind in You 79
- The Mystery of Job 81
- The Disciple's Life 84
- They Gave It All 87
- For All the World to See 88

The Blessing – Mountaintop or Valley 91

Week 1

Know What You Believe

Happy are the people whose strength is in You, whose hearts are set on pilgrimage. ⁶As they pass through the Valley of Tears, they make it a source of springwater; even the autumn rain will cover it will blessings. ⁷They go from strength to strength; each appears before God in Zion. Psalm 84:5-7

This valley of tears is a place that we have all visited at some point in our lives. We don't have to look far to find stories of brokenness, pain, and suffering. The world news covers tragic events almost daily, and our national and local news channels are filled with stories of loss and destruction. If the truth is told, and those cameras were filming in our homes, they would find hurt, disappointment and pain. Things happen in life that hurt, that take our breath away and make us wonder if we can even go on.

A beloved son commits suicide, a mom loses two of her children in a horrific car accident, a cherished husband drowns, an accidental gunshot steals the life of a child, a heart-attack takes the life of a husband and father, Alzheimer's robs a family of their precious mom.

Those are events from people I know, and if time allowed, I could share other stories, as I am sure that you could as well. Our coffee would grow cold if we sat and shared the many trials of our souls. We could describe first-hand the rejection, humiliation, abandonment, sickness, pain, loss, grief, persecution, unfairness, injustice and emptiness which fill this valley of tears.

A sudden step into a painful dark valley is shocking and can be very confusing. It is normal for a flood of emotions and sorrow is expected. But I have noticed among my friends and family that have walked through various valleys filled with many tears that some walk through the valley, believing and trusting God to get them through it and others, who also know God, grow bitter and angry and turn away from Him.

I began to wonder what caused the difference was between the two outcomes. I began to wonder what is happening in our minds when we take that unexpected step from a normal everyday journey into the dark valley place?

I thought of what it is like for us when we experience darkness, sickness, pain, or confusing situations in our normal everyday life and how those events affect our emotions and decisions.

For instance, has darkness ever caused you to be disoriented or confused? Maybe you've gotten lost while driving at night because you missed the visual reminders that usually guided your way? Or maybe like my friend Leah Turner sudden darkness has confused and frightened you. Leah was in her nineties and helping with our summer Vacation Bible School. One particular evening a group of us were making snacks in the kitchen area of our school gymnasium when the power went out. The darkness surprised us, but thankfully emergency lights kicked on giving us enough light to finish. We laughed in the kitchen and carried on until we heard a faraway desperate voice calling for help. I followed the cries for help to the pitch-black girl's bathroom. Leah was in there and was terrified thinking she'd gone blind. When she was plunged into sudden darkness, she became confused, fearful and irrational.

I also realized that darkness can create shadows which distort reality. Shadows are distorted reflections – they are not real objects. I have a wall-sized mirror in my home with windows across from it. Many times I have been frightened by my own image reflected from the mirror to the window and vice versa.

The Blessing

In thinking through normal everyday life and bumps in the road and how those experiences affect our lives, I realized that our perspective can be changed. Have you ever been afflicted by a nasty bout of the stomach flu? If you're like me, within a few hours you don't care if you live or die, you just want the misery to go away. It's easy to lose perspective on the big picture and develop a tunnel vision in moments of pain and suffering.

I realized if it's easy to become confused, disoriented, and lose perspective when I experience daily hardships, then it must be overwhelming when we find ourselves in a dark valley of tears. I understand the difficulty that surrounds making rational, decisions when traumatized and I began to wonder if it was possible to prepare ahead of time for the valley. Could we study people in the Bible who had been asked by God to walk through these very difficult valley places and learn the terrain ahead of time?

What does God teach us about these valleys?

Happy are the people whose strength is in You, whose hearts are set on pilgrimage. ⁶As they pass through the Valley of Tears, they make it a source of springwater; even the autumn rain will cover it will blessings. ⁷They go from strength to strength; each appears before God in Zion. Psalm 84:5-7

A casual observation of Psalm 84:5-7 tells us the following true things:

- Travelers through the valley can find joy when they make God their source of strength.
- The valley is meant to be traveled through, not settled in. It's a pilgrimage, not a destination.
- The valley can be a source of spring water. It can be a place of renewal.
- The autumn rains will cover the dry, parched valley bringing blessing! These rains replenish the soil, preparing it for future harvests.
- The valley doesn't have to make us weak; it can make us stronger.

These are truths about the valley that I want to understand a head of time.

If I had told my friend Leah that the lights would go out when she was in the bathroom, it still would have been very dark in there, and she still would have had to feel her way to walk through the darkness, but the fear that enveloped her would have been eliminated. She would have been able to keep the right perspective in the midst of the trial.

God has given us many examples in the Bible of men and women who endured great trials and sacrifices. Death, suffering, and pain have come into this world as a result of sin. These were not part of the perfect plan that God offered to man; they are, however, the result of the plan that man chose to take (Romans 5:12). This knowledge shouldn't fill our hearts with fear or despair because in John 16:33, Jesus said, **"I have told you these things so that in Me you may have peace. You will have suffering in this world. Be courageous! I have conquered the world."**

We have this promise of God's presence and His peace along with many other promises just like it in the Bible. If we know that He is with us, what happens in that sudden moment of trial that causes us to fear? Why is it that feelings of despair, anger and hopelessness can overwhelm us and bring confusion and fear?

We have an enemy.

Satan would love to isolate you in your place of pain. One of his most successful tools in our suffering is to convince us to focus all of our attention on the problem. Let me illustrate. Imagine that you have fallen and severely injured your leg. I am talking about a bloody, skin peeled back, bone exposed, kind of wound. It is excruciatingly painful and just when you think it can't hurt any worse, someone begins to talk to you.

> "Don't touch it! Don't move! Just sit there. If you move, it will just bleed more. Look at how deep that cut is! I don't know how you can stand the pain. Is that the bone is sticking out? I bet you broke it. What happened anyway? Did you have any warning? Did someone push you? Is this someone's fault? You thought he was your friend? Couldn't he have prevented this? Look at that puddle of blood. That is a terrible wound; I don't know how you are ever going to recover. This is far worse than you ever imagined. Are you all alone? I don't think anyone cares about you. I would be crying too. This is terrible! I doubt you'll ever be the same again."

That's an example of the kinds of alienating words that the Devil likes to speak into your soul when you find yourself plunged into a trial that takes your breath away. He wants you to focus on the pain, on the horror of it all and the injustice. He wants you to feel alone and abandoned by a God that could not possibly be good.

Imagine the same injured leg scenario with someone saying this:

> "I'm sorry that you're hurting. Here, let me wipe the dirt off. I need to apply pressure to the wound so that I can stop the bleeding. I know this hurts you, but it will be better if you let me help you. It may take a few minutes to stop this hemorrhage, but I'll sit with you and talk to you until it is safe to move. When we do start walking, you can lean on me. I'll bear your weight. Until then rest your head on me, I'll stay with you."

In reality, we have both of those voices speaking to us in our pain.

- The devil doesn't want you to get better. He wants you to dwell in the darkness of the valley of tears forever, so He seeks to isolate you from the One who truly loves and wants to strengthen you. Did you know that the word *devil* in the Greek means *false accuser*? Did you know that it also implies *divider*? The devil wants to separate us from God, and he will cast either himself or something in between to cause division.[1] When a trial or period of suffering comes into our lives, the devil delights in keeping us away from the Father. He smirks and whispers accusations against the character of God. The devil would rather keep us focused on our pain; if we are self-focused, we won't be God-focused. He loves it when we lose sight of God and feel angry and alone!

- On the other hand, Jesus sits beside you; He won't leave you alone. He patiently waits for us to let go of the wound so that he can gently tend it. He won't peel your fingers back; He won't force you to accept His help, He just keeps speaking to you and waiting.

---

[1] Zodhiates, Spiros, ed. *The Hebrew-Greek Key Word Study Bible* (Chattanooga, TN: AMG Publishers, 1996), #1228, page 1821

I brought you from the ends of the earth and called you from its farthest corners. I said to you: You are My servant; I have chosen you and not rejected you. ¹⁰Do not fear for I am with you; do not be afraid, for I am your God. I will strengthen you; I will help you; I will hold on to you with My righteous right hand. ¹¹Be sure that all who are enraged against you will be ashamed and disgraced; those who contend with you will become as nothing and will perish. ¹²You will look for those who contend with you, but you will not find them. Those who war against you will become absolutely nothing. ¹³For I, the LORD your God, hold your right hand and say to you: Do not fear, I will help you. Isaiah 41:9-13

I am not downplaying the pain. I know what it is like to have days of tears, followed by more days of tears; to be so caught up in the pain that you can barely think. But in those moments, you can look down at your hand and know that your God is holding you with His righteous right hand and that He loves you and desires to strengthen and guide you.

When you are led to the valley of tears, you need to decide whose voice we will trust in the darkness. One option is to listen to the voice that tells you to focus on the pain, the lying voice which says you're alone and not likely to recover. The other option is to turn to the One whose voice you know; the voice who has spoken to your heart on many previous occasions. The voice of truth, the voice of the One you trust.

Get to know the voice of God! Get to know His heart, His character. When blackness settles in around me, and I cannot see the way to take, I reach for His hand and let Him lead me on.

The example we have of Jesus when He was here on earth is that He drew near to His Father. On many occasions in the Gospels, we read about Jesus praying. We see him withdrawing from large crowds to spend time with His Father. He would often pray long into the night. After He had been busy doing the work of His Father, he would retreat to talk to Him. Hebrews 5:7 says that Jesus offered up prayers with loud cries and tears! We see that Jesus drew near to the Holy One, to the One whose character He knew to be true. He endured injustices in life because He knew that His Father, the Creator God, was at work completing something far more significant than could be understood by simply looking at the present hour, day or even year. Jesus trusted that the One who was guiding Him knew the way that they were going.

If we are going to trust His voice in the dark valley, if we are going to walk by faith and not by sight, then we need to draw near to Him. We need to get to know Him. We need to learn all that we can about Him in the light of the day before we need to recognize His voice in the valley of darkness.

What can we know about our God? What does Scripture reveal to us about Him?

Our God is:

> **Omniscient** (knows all things): Psalm 147:4-5; Hebrews 4:13; Matthew 10:29-30
> **Omnipotent** (all powerful): Genesis 1:1; Jeremiah 32:27
> **Omnipresence** (present everywhere): Psalm 139:7-12; Isaiah 23:24; Matthew 18:20
> **Self-existent**: Exodus 3:13-14
> **Everlasting:** Psalm 90:2, Isaiah 40:28
> **Wise:** Proverbs 3:19; Romans 11:33
> **Unchanging:** Acts 1:11; Hebrews 1:10-12; Hebrews 13:8

Sovereign: Is. 46:9-11; Psalm 135:6
Love: John 3:16, I John 4:19, I Corinthians 13
Holy: Isaiah 48:17; 1 Peter 1:16
True: John 14:6; Titus 1:2; Hebrews 6:18; Revelation 19:11
Merciful: Psalm 136:1; Ps. 103:17
Good: Nahum 1:7
Gracious: Ps. 145:8

I may not understand all that is happening in my life, but this one thing I know; My God is an all-powerful God who knows all things, and He is with me. He doesn't change, and He is wise and good. He is full of mercy, and He is loving, holy and true. He offers Himself to me as my Father, and I may not understand Him, but I trust Him for He is without a doubt trustworthy!

We need to know Him now so that we are not deceived in the darkness by the voice of the one who speaks lies.

This week in our homework lessons we will be searching the Scriptures and collecting as many verses as we can about our Great God! We are not looking to just gain head knowledge about God. We need to meditate on these truths and plant them deep in our hearts so that on the day we find ourselves in the valley of tears, we will not believe the lies that the devil will whisper to us. Instead, we will believe what is true about God, and we will hold fast to His hand.

The key to making a pilgrimage through the valley of tears is to draw near to the source of our strength. To drink deeply from the One who promises in John 4 to be our source of living water. His presence will distinguish us from those around us who do not have God. We have Him! We should not suffer as those who have no hope; we have the blessing of His presence and the promise that He will help us. Redirect your focus to Him; rehearse what you know to be true. This is not a promise that the pain will disappear, but it is a promise that we won't lose our way in the darkness and that our traveling companion will comfort and guide us through the valley places.

This first lesson is about establishing what we know to be true, creating a compass point of true north in our hearts so that when we find ourselves in a dark place, we don't wander and lose our way. We discover God in our valley of tears and according to Psalm 84:5-7, when we know Him we are strengthened, and we can even experience a soul joy.

Few people understand how anyone can be happy in the valley place, but the Bible says that when we know God, there is a joy that transcends even our own understanding. The homework this week explores some of these remarkable truths about our great God. Etch them upon your heart and mind so that they become as familiar to you as your own face in the mirror. You want to be able to say with absolute confidence, "These things I know to be true. My God is . . . ."

Next week we will begin to explore the universal question that people ask when they find themselves in a valley of tears. "Why?"

We are never promised that we will understand all that God does. In fact, Isaiah 55:9 says, **"For as heaven is higher than earth, so My ways are higher than your ways, and My thoughts than your thoughts."**

The Blessing

Romans 11:33 says, **"Oh, the depth of the riches both of the wisdom and the knowledge of God! How unsearchable His judgments and untraceable His ways!"** God is unfathomable. He is the Creator, and we are the created. He is the Potter, we are the clay. We cannot comprehend Him or His ways.

We will see examples of people in the Bible who endured great suffering without understanding why God had allowed the great trial into their life. They chose to trust God not because they knew the "why" but rather because they knew the "who."

If we only follow God when we understand what He's doing, and it makes sense to us, we are walking by sight, and not by faith. God is so much greater than we can see and understand. He is the Almighty Creator God who has given Himself for us. He is trustworthy!

We need to know what we believe and believe what we know.

But the people who know their God will be strong and take action. Daniel 11:32b

Dear Father, dark valleys are hard places. You know that we are made of flesh and that we don't have much strength, so when we find ourselves in a dark valley place, help us to know that we can be confident that you are at work completing something we don't understand. Help us to know what we believe and then believe what we know. We know that we can trust your sovereignty, your goodness, and your mercy. We know that you love us with a Father's love and that your presence comforts our hearts and brings peace. You have never promised that life won't hurt, but you have promised to be with us and to strengthen and guide us. Help us to trust you in dark places. Help us to know your voice so well that we will never be deceived by the voice of your enemy. We hold out our hands to you and invite you to take hold of them. Whom do we have in heaven but You? **Whom do I have in heaven but You? And I desire nothing on earth but You. ^{26}My flesh and my heart may fail, but God is the strength of my heart, my portion forever. Psalm 73:25-26**

Day 1

He Does Not Change

Jesus Christ is the same yesterday, today, and forever. Hebrews 13:8

When I have faced unsettling news or unexpected circumstances, sometimes I have said out loud, "If I trusted that God was directing my footsteps yesterday, then I have to believe He is directing them today also. He is still trustworthy." God does not change. His character is immutable, meaning it cannot change. **Every generous act and every perfect gift is from above, coming down from the Father of lights; with Him, there is no variation or shadow cast by turning** (James 1:17). What we know to be true about God in Scripture is still true today. He has not changed, nor will He ever. His character and His attributes remain the same. Because He does not change He is faithful. What He has said, He will do.

The God that we read about in Genesis, who with a breath spoke the worlds into existence, who created man out of the dust of the ground and breathed into his nostrils the breath of life, doesn't change. We can thoroughly trust in this God who rules the world in power and authority; He has not grown weak, and things have not spun out of His control. This God, who has loved us with an everlasting love and pursued the heart of mankind, was willing to provide a way for our redemption at the highest cost to Himself, the sacrifice of his One and Only Son Jesus. *That* is what we know to be true about God.

So what does the work of this unchanging, faithful, all-powerful God look like in scripture?

Psalm 115:3 Our God is in heaven and does whatever He _____

Isaiah 45:5-7 I am the LORD, and there is no other; _____
I will strengthen you, though you do not know Me, ⁶so that all may know from the rising of the sun to its setting that there is no one but Me. I am the LORD, and there is no other. ⁷I form light and create darkness, I make success and create disaster; I, the LORD, do all these things.

Isaiah 45:12 I made the earth, and created man on it. It was My hands that stretched out the heavens, and I commanded all their host.

Isaiah 46:9-11 Remember what happened long ago, for I am God, and there is no other; I am God, and no one is like Me. ¹⁰I declare the end from the beginning, and from long ago what is not yet done, saying: _____
¹¹I call a bird of prey from the east, a man for My purpose from a far country. Yes, I have spoken;
_____

Daniel 4:35 All the inhabitants of the earth are counted as nothing, and He does what He wants with the army of heaven and the inhabitants of the earth. _____
_____

Isaiah 64:8 Yet LORD, You are our Father; we are the _____ **, and You are our;** _____
we all are the work of Your Hands.

The Blessing

Job 23:13-15 But He is _____ ; who can oppose Him? He does what He _____. ¹⁴He will_____ accomplish what He has decreed for me, and He has many more things like these in mind. ¹⁵Therefore I am terrified in His presence; when I consider this, I am afraid of Him.

Job 42:2 I know that You can do _____ and no plan of Yours can be _____.

Wow! No plan of God's can be thwarted. He will do as He pleases and He will do as He has decreed. He is immoveable, and that is a great comfort to me; I know that God's plan for my life cannot be altered because of another person, event, sickness, etc. God's will for my life will be accomplished just as He has decreed. This gives me great confidence that while I may not like all the various events in my life, I know that my unchanging, faithful, powerful, Sovereign God has ordained them for my days.

For some of us, it is this very knowledge that nothing is too difficult for God that frustrates or angers us the most. We **know** that He could answer our prayers and bring relief to the situation that we are in, and we feel hurt or angry when he does not answer our prayers the way we think He should. Romans 9 addresses this when Paul describes God's work through the ages and His choice to exalt some and humble others, and God's decisions to demonstrate compassion on some and not others. Romans 9:20-23 says, **"Who in the world do you think you are to second-guess God? Do you for one moment suppose any of us knows enough to call God into question? Clay doesn't talk back to the fingers that mold it, saying, 'Why did you shape me like this?' Isn't it obvious that a potter has a perfect right to shape one lump of clay into a vase for holding flowers and another into a pot for cooking beans? If God needs one style of pottery especially designed to show his angry displeasure and another style carefully crafted to show his glorious goodness, isn't that all right?"** (The Message)

As a Holy, Sovereign, Creator God, He can do, and He does all that pleases Him.

Before you let this ruffle your feathers, read Isaiah 53:10. This verse describes something that God did that pleased Him. **"It pleased the Lord to bruise him; he hath put him to grief: when thou shalt make his soul an offering for sin, he shall see his seed, he shall prolong his days, and the pleasure of the Lord shall prosper in his hand."** (KJV) It was God's will and His pleasure to allow the suffering of Jesus because, in God's sovereign wisdom, He knew that the redemption of souls was at stake. This is not to say that God *enjoyed* watching His Son suffer! God forbid! That is contrary to the love of God, but at the completion of that suffering, there was something of unimaginable worth to God – the redemption of man! There was something really big at stake!! Praise God that it pleased Him to order the steps of Jesus and that the Lord Jesus willingly yielded to God's sovereign plan!

You can trust the Sovereign character of God in your valley place. If your place of suffering seems unfair and unbearable, fix your eyes on Jesus!

Hebrews 12: 1-3 Therefore since we also have such a large cloud of witnesses surrounding us, let us lay aside every weight and the sin that so easily ensnares us, and run with endurance the race that lies before us, ² _____ , the source and perfecter of our faith, _____ endured a cross and despised the shame, and has sat down at the right hand of God's throne. ³For consider Him who endured such hostility from sinners against Himself so that you won't grow weary and lose heart.

He can do all things, and He will accomplish His purposes in you and through you!

Being reminded of the sovereignty of God also reminds us that we are the work of His hand and, like Moses, Isaiah, Daniel, Ezekiel, John and others who have come face to face with God in scripture, we fall to our knees in terror of His Glory and we worship Him. We cannot look upon the Glory of Almighty God and stand with our fists raised in anger or despair because when we see Him, we also see ourselves and we kneel before His Glory desperate for His Mercy and Grace.

In the book, The Lion, The Witch & The Wardrobe, I have always liked Mr. Beaver's answer to Lucy's question about Aslan.

> Lucy: "Is he – quite safe?"
>
> "Safe?" said Mr. Beaver, "Who said anything about safe? **'Course he isn't safe. But he's good.** He's the King, I tell you."[1]

We can rest confidently in the power and sovereignty of Almighty Creator God who can do as He pleases and accomplishes all that He sets out to do. He isn't tame! But thankfully, tomorrow we will add to this collection of verses that describe Almighty God as our Father. We will learn the amazing truth that God's Sovereignty never contradicts his paternity! He is our Sovereign Father! Praise God!

> **"Look, I am the LORD, the God of all flesh. Is anything too difficult for Me?" Jeremiah 32:27**

Just between you and me, God _____
_____
_____
_____

Day 2

He is My Father

For you did not receive a spirit of slavery to fall back into fear, but you received the Spirit of adoption, by whom we cry out, "Abba, Father!" Romans 8:15

Did you know that the people in the Old Testament did not have the privilege of approaching God as their Father? They could only approach Him through the mediator of a priest. It is only because of Jesus and His sacrificial death on the cross and His resurrection that we have been offered forgiveness of sins and a restored relationship with God. We approach our Holy God, dressed in the righteous robes of His Son, Jesus Christ, and it is because of this relationship that we have with Jesus that we have been adopted into God's family and we can call God, "Abba, Father!"

"Abba" is a Greek word that was used as a paternal term of endearment, like we would use the word "Daddy." Jesus called God the Father, "Daddy." Jesus is recorded in Scripture as talking to God many

---

[1] Lewis, Clive Staples, *The Lion, The Witch & The Wardrobe* (Harper Collins, *1950)*

The Blessing

times in prayer, but we see an especially tender example of this communication just hours before Jesus would be led to the cross. Jesus, in great anguish, knelt alone in the garden and talked with His Father.

Mark 14:36 And He said, _____ All things are possible for You. Take this cup away from Me. Nevertheless, _____

God's will for His only begotten Son, Jesus, the second member of the Trinity of the Godhead, was to pass through a valley of great suffering.

God was not angry or disappointed at His Son's request. He wasn't upset that Jesus was distressed to the point of sweating blood. This was a great trial; a game-changer. Would Jesus, when faced with unimaginable suffering, choose to trust God or would He refuse the valley journey that God had ordained for Him? Jesus knelt in great distress and asked God if there was any other way possible to accomplish the work, but He yielded His will to the will of the Father. Jesus trusted the character of His Father, knowing that the sovereign plans of God were good and that God would strengthen Him for the task.

What possible good could come out of false accusations, a horrific beating, humiliation and excruciating death of being nailed to a cross? When we only look at the circumstances as we can see and understand them, it is impossible to see any good. But rest assured, our Almighty God, who knows the beginning from the end, whose ways are unfathomable to us, can redeem even the most painful of experiences and allow a harvest of righteousness!

The harvest of righteousness that came from Jesus' willingness to trust a sovereign Father who loved Him was the salvation of souls, including yours and mine! When we accept that God has pursued the sinful heart of man and made a way of salvation and forgiveness available to us through the shed blood of His Son, we are forgiven and clothed in righteousness. The Spirit of God comes to dwell within us, and in this restored place, we are His children, and we can boldly approach the throne of God.

Hebrews 4:16 _____

_____

_____

We don't need to approach God through a Priest anymore! Jesus came as our priest and mediator. He became the sacrifice so that we could become sons of God and approach Him as children.

Matthew 7:11 If you then, who are evil, know how to _____ to your children, how much more will your _____ in heaven _____ things to those who ask Him!

Jesus is teaching a large audience of people about God, His Father, in this passage. He compares earthly fathers who love their kids and give good gifts to them, to the Heavenly Father who is infinitely good and who gives good things to those who ask Him.

We like this verse, but I think it sometimes confuses and frustrates people. Often we want to interpret this verse to mean that we will receive only good (*pleasant and desirable*) things from God and that if we ask Him for good things, He will give them to us. That interpretation treats God like a benevolent grandpa, who spoils his grandchildren by giving them everything they ask for. We claim this verse and then express our anger or disappointment when God doesn't grant our requests. We stomp our feet in a temper tantrum and rage that God cannot be trusted because He didn't give us the things we wanted.

Did Jesus ask that His suffering be removed? _____ Did God remove it? _____
Did God give Jesus a good thing? _____

The salvation of the souls of mankind would definitely be a good thing, but it would only come after the suffering of Jesus. Undoubtedly God's gift of breaking the curse of sin and death was a good thing! Did this good thing happen in a pleasant, comfortable, easy-to-handle manner?

If we look strictly at the empirical evidence we might come to the conclusion that God wasn't trustworthy; His Son was in need, His Son asked for deliverance, and God chose not to deliver him from suffering. But before we can make such a harsh theological judgment about God, we must begin not with the things that we see, but rather with the things that we know to be true about God. We look at the attributes of God in Scripture. He is all-powerful. He is sovereign. He knows all things. He is everywhere. He is good. He is Holy. He is merciful. He is love, etc. We need to start with what we know about God, and then we can look at the evidence of the things seen in our circumstances.

When we know what we believe about God, then we can, like Jesus, approach God and ask if there is another way, but yield ourselves to His wisdom. We may not understand the circumstances any better, but our conclusion will be more accurate.

"God, we do not understand how this can be good or how it can be used for good in your kingdom. It hurts terribly, and if there is any way that you can remove it and still accomplish your purpose, please do so. If I must endure this, then I trust you and yield my will to yours; may you accomplish all that you desire through me and in me."

"Thank you, Jesus, for showing us by your example that your sovereign Father was trustworthy in the darkest of valleys and thank you that because of your obedience we can call Him Father also!"

But when the completion of the time came, God sent His Son, born of a woman, born under the law, ⁵to redeem those under the law, so that we might receive adoption as sons. ⁶And because you are sons, God has sent the Spirit of His Son into our hearts, crying, "*Abba*, Father!" ⁷So you are no longer a slave, but a son; and if a son, then an heir through God. Galatians 4:4-7

I Peter 1:3-12 tells us that even the angels desire to look into this great mystery of salvation and adoption. It is something that baffles their understanding. It is indeed a marvelous thing that we should be called sons of God and to be His heirs.

God's paternity is like a glove of love over his sovereign hand.

Just between you and me, God: _____
_____
_____
_____
_____
_____

Day 3

He Loves Me

For God so loved the world, that He gave His only begotten Son that whosoever believeth in Him, should not perish but have everlasting life. John 3:16 (KJV)

This is probably the most well-known Scripture verse in the entire world because it succinctly expresses the heart of our God and the good news that He made a way for salvation of men. This is an amazing kind of love. Our sin had estranged us from God, but according to Romans 5:5-8, God demonstrated His great love for us by sending Jesus to die for us while we were still stuck in our trespasses and sins! John 15:13 says, **"No one has greater love than this, that someone would lay down his life for his friends."** Jesus laid down His life for the very people who were taking His life!

Read Ephesians 2:1-10. It is a beautiful picture of God's redeeming love.

And you were dead in your trespasses and sins ²in which you previously walked according to this worldly age, according to the ruler of the atmospheric domain, the spirit now working in the disobedient. ³We too all previously lived among them in our fleshly desires, carrying out the inclinations of our flesh and thoughts, and by nature, we were children under wrath, as the others were also. ⁴But God, who is abundant in mercy, because of His great love that He had for us, ⁵made us alive with the Messiah even though we were dead in trespasses. By grace, you are saved! ⁶He also raised us up with Him and seated us with Him in the heavens, in Christ Jesus, ⁷so that in the coming ages He might display the immeasurable riches of His grace in His kindness to us in Christ Jesus. ⁸For by grace you are saved through faith, and this is not from yourselves; it is God's gift— ⁹not from works so that no one can boast. ¹⁰For we are His creation—created in Christ Jesus for good works, which God prepared ahead of time so that we should walk in them.

According to this passage, in verses 4-5, do we have to be right and get our act together before God makes us His child? _____

Can we in any way affect His great demonstration of love? Is it possible to live according to our fleshly desires to the degree that God won't offer salvation to us? Is the grace that God offers to us based on our goodness or God's great love? _____

Verse six says that Christ Jesus has raised us up and seated us where? _____

Since we are all still living here on earth, what can that possibly mean? It means that our citizenship is in heaven. Heaven is now our home. Imagine that! Yes, we live here on planet earth, but we are foreigners, just pilgrims passing through on our way home! God has paid our way! He has protected us from the penalty of sin which is death and an eternity spent in a place called hell.

What is God's purpose in this great demonstration of love?

Verse 7 _____

Verse 10 _____

Let's collect some verses that describe this great love that God has for us. The verses are typed out for you followed by some blank lines for writing. After you have read the verse, see if you can personalize it by paraphrasing it. I will give you an example for the first one.

I will sing about the LORD's faithful love forever; with my mouth, I will proclaim Your faithfulness to all generations. Psalm 89:1

"Lord, your faithful love, which is demonstrated in your loving kindness and mercy, causes my heart to burst forth in song. In a generation that knows what unfaithfulness is, I want to tell them all about you!"

Get the idea? There isn't a right or wrong – it is letting God's words flow back to Him in the form of praise or petition.

Then the LORD passed in front of him and proclaimed: Yahweh—Yahweh is a compassionate and gracious God, slow to anger and rich in faithful love and truth… Exodus 34:6

_____
_____

Remember, LORD, Your compassion and Your faithful love, for they have existed from antiquity. Psalm 25:6

_____
_____

LORD, do not withhold Your compassion from me; Your constant love and truth will always guard me. Psalm 40:11

_____
_____

But I will sing of Your strength and will joyfully proclaim Your faithful love in the morning. For You have been a stronghold for me, a refuge in my day of trouble. Psalm 59:16

_____
_____

Give thanks to the LORD, for He is good; His faithful love endures forever. Psalm 107:1

_____
_____

God's love was revealed among us in this way: God sent His One and Only Son into the world so that we might live through Him. I John 4:9

_____
_____

We serve a faithful God. Sin separated us from God, and we were unfaithful to Him, but He loved us and pursued the heart of man and made a way for us to be restored to Him. His love is faithful! Even, as we are told in II Timothy 2:13, **"if we are faithless, He remains faithful, for He cannot deny Himself."**

The Blessing

Our sovereign, all-powerful God, who does not change and cannot be hindered in His work, is a good Father who demonstrates His faithful love to us by providing salvation through the sacrifice of His Son. He met our greatest need and according to Philippians 4:19, He will continue to meet all our needs. This Father God, who is my stronghold and my place of refuge, is forever faithful to me. The works that He has prepared for me to do since before the foundation of the world (Ephesians 2:10) are good, because He is good. He is trustworthy; God's love never fails.

My lips will glorify You because Your faithful love is better than life. Psalm 63:3

Just between you and me, God: _____

_____

_____

_____

_____

Day 4

He Is With Me

I will never leave you or forsake you. Hebrews 13:5b

This week, we are collecting truths in Scripture that highlight the character and attributes of God so that when we find ourselves in a valley of tears and we do not understand why and don't know what to do, we can look to what we know to be true about God and set our hearts and our minds on Him. So far this week we have been reminded of God's sovereignty; He can do anything. We have also looked at the His paternity; He has adopted us into His family. He is a Father who loves us with a faithful love. Today we will spend a few minutes capturing the amazing truth that He is always with us.

In the Garden of Eden at the fall of man, the Spirit of God departed from the presence of man. The Spirit of Life that had filled the heart of man departed and in its place was sin and death. The intimate relationship that Adam and Eve had experienced with God was gone because sin had separated God and man. That day brought an emptiness of soul that had never been experienced before.

Because of God's great love for mankind, he made a promise in Genesis chapter 3 that he would one day send a Savior, the seed of the woman, to crush the head of the deceiver and break the curse of sin. This was a promise made from a heart of love; sin had separated man from God, but it wouldn't always be that way. One day, the promised one would come, and He would make a way for man to know the presence of God again in a real and personal way.

Matthew 1:23 "See, the virgin will become pregnant and give birth to a son, and they will name Him Immanuel, which is translated " _____ ."

The long-awaited promised One; He came, and He lived a perfect, sinless life here on earth and was willing to be offered up as the sacrifice for all the sins of mankind. His death, burial, and resurrection brought the means of having our sins forgiven so that we could be restored in our relationship with God; His spirit could dwell within us again! We could know and experience life. Eternal life! Death was defeated!

In a lesson on the shield of faith in the Dressed for the Business at Hand Bible study, we spent a day exploring verses that described the presence of God in our lives.

We saw in Psalm 139:5 that he **encircles** us and that His hand is **upon** us. In Exodus 14:19-20, we saw God **before** the Israelites, as well as **behind** them and **between** them and the enemy. In Joshua 2:11, we saw the presence of God described as being **above** and **below**. Psalm 125:2 says that God **surrounds** us.

God is around, above, below, before, behind, between and surrounding us!

And since the cross…
Colossians 1:27 God wanted to make known to those among the Gentiles the glorious wealth of this mystery, which is Christ_____ , the hope of glory.

Ever since the Garden of Eden and the entrance of sin into this world, mankind has craved the presence of God in His life. Blaise Pascal, a 16th-century scientist, and philosopher is quoted as saying, "There is a God-shaped vacuum in the heart of every man which cannot be filled by any created thing, but only by God, the Creator made known through Jesus."

There is within the heart of every man a sense of something missing. Man will try to fill that emptiness with many things, but only the presence of God in His life will bring the end to his life-long search. It is God's amazing love toward us that caused Him to move with compassion in sending His Son to be the Savior of the world so that with the forgiveness of our sins His presence could be restored to dwell in us!

This fact alone is one of the most stunning revelations about our salvation. This knowledge that God's presence is within us, that He indwells us as His temple (I Corinthians 3:16, 6:19), should bring great comfort in our trials. The enemy wants us to believe that God has abandoned us; that He is gone and we are alone. Satan lies to us, and in those dark valley moments when we cannot see the hand of God, we may be tempted to believe the lie unless we understand the truth that His presence is within us and wherever we are, He is there with us! He cannot leave Himself. He has no desire to leave us; we belong to Him, and He loves us with the love of a Father (John 10: 28-31, Hebrews 13:5)!

What then are we to say about these things? If God is for us, who is against us? ³²He did not even spare His own Son, but offered Him up for us all; how will He not also with Him grant us everything? ³³Who can bring an accusation against God's elect? God is the One who justifies. ³⁴Who is the one who condemns? Christ Jesus is the One who died, but even more, has been raised; He also is at the right hand of God and intercedes for us. ³⁵Who can separate us from the love of Christ? Can affliction or anguish or persecution or famine or nakedness or danger or sword? ³⁶As it is written: Because of You, we are being put to death all day long; we are counted as sheep to be slaughtered. ³⁷No, in all these things we are more than victorious through Him who loved us. ³⁸For I am persuaded that neither death nor life, nor angels nor rulers, nor things present nor things to come, nor powers, ³⁹nor height, nor depth, nor any other created thing will have the power to separate us from the love of God that is in Christ Jesus our Lord! Romans 8:31-39

Do **not** believe the enemy; God is all around you, and He is within you!

The Blessing

In II Kings 6:8-17, we find a remarkable account of Elisha, the prophet of God, and one of his servants. The nation of Israel was at war with the neighboring nation of Aram, and during the night, the enemy's army had surrounded the city in which Elisha stayed. Elisha's servant woke up in the morning and was filled with fear when he saw the soldiers. He was terrified and didn't know what to do. **Elisha said, "Don't be afraid, for those who are with us outnumber those who are with them."** I am sure this confused the servant as he could clearly see that the number of enemy soldiers outstripped the number of fighting men in the city. **Then Elisha prayed, "LORD, please open his eyes and let him see." So the LORD opened the servant's eyes. He looked and saw that the mountain was covered with horses and chariots of fire all around Elisha.**

When you are walking in the Valley of Tears, do not trust your emotions. We perceive and look with human eyes that cannot accurately see or understand. Do not let fear fill your heart; instead, cry out to your all-powerful God who loves you with Fatherly love and who promises to never leave you nor forsake you. When you cannot see the way to take, you can trust that your Father is by your side and if you allow Him, He will take hold of your hand and lead you on.

Isaiah 41:13 _____
_____
_____
_____

I will be with you when you pass through the waters, and when you pass through the rivers, they will not overwhelm you. You will not be scorched when you walk through the fire, and the flame will not burn you. Isaiah 43:2

Just between you and me, God: _____
_____
_____
_____
_____

Day 5

He Brings Peace

Don't worry about anything, but in everything, through prayer and petition with thanksgiving, let your requests be made known to God. ⁷And the peace of God, which surpasses every thought, will guard your hearts and your minds in Christ Jesus. Philippians 4:6-7

I love these verses! But I am wondering if you know why the Apostle Paul told the people that they didn't need to worry about anything? Read Philippians 4:4-5 and fill in the blank.

Philippians 4:4-5 Rejoice in the Lord always. I will say it again: Rejoice! ⁵Let your graciousness be known to everyone. _____ .

You see, it is the presence of God in our lives that is the source of our peace! The Greek word used in this verse for peace is "eirene" and it is defined as "being at rest, the absence of strife."[2] Strife is a state of division and contention. It is a sharp differing of opinion. God, the Almighty powerful One, who loves us with a Fatherly love, has drawn near and His presence brings peace. His presence stills the voice of the accuser when he stirs up contentious lies that could spur thoughts of worry and fear. We rest in the presence of God.

This is the message of the Gospel!

Acts 10:36 He sent the message to the sons of Israel, proclaiming the good news of _____ _____—He is Lord of all.

"How beautiful are the feet of those who preach the gospel of peace, who bring glad tidings of good things!" Romans 10:15b (NKJV)

When Christ came, He proclaimed the good news of peace to you who were far away and peace to those who were near. Ephesians 2:17

This peace of God comes only as a result of our being reconciled to God through the work that Jesus accomplished on the cross.

Romans 5:1-2 Therefore, since we have been declared righteous by faith, we have _____ _____ ²Also through Him, we have obtained _____ by faith into this grace in which we stand, and we rejoice in the hope of the glory of God.

These verses are awesome! We have a relationship of peace with God; we have been given the right to have access to Him. This access had been missing since the fall of man in Genesis chapter 3. And if that isn't awesome enough, the passage continues with a message of hope and encouragement to all of us who live in this broken world and experience its trials.

And not only that, but we also rejoice in our afflictions, because we know that affliction produces endurance, ⁴endurance produces proven character, and proven character produces hope. ⁵This hope does not disappoint because God's love has been poured out in our hearts through the Holy Spirit who was given to us. Romans 5:3-4

We have peace with God; He is with us and not only that, we can rejoice in our afflictions because we know that the affliction is producing something of greater worth in our lives!

Hebrews 12:1-3 Therefore since we also have such a large cloud of witnesses surrounding us, let us lay aside every weight and the sin that so easily ensnares us, and run with endurance the race that lies before us, ² _____ _____ _____ and has sat down at the right hand of God's throne. ³For consider _____ who endured such _____ from sinners against Himself, so that _____ _____ .

---

[2] Zodhiates, Spiros, ed. *The Hebrew-Greek Key Word Study Bible* (Chattanooga, TN: AMG Publishers, 1996) #1515, page 1829

The Blessing

When we are in that valley of tears, we rest knowing that we have the presence of Almighty God with us. Romans 8:26 tells us that when we are overwhelmed in our weakness and don't even know how to talk to God about it, the Spirit of God who lives within us prays on our behalf to our Father God.

In the same way, the Spirit also joins to help in our weakness, because we do not know what to pray for as we should, but the Spirit Himself intercedes for us with unspoken groanings. Romans 8:26

Our God is not like the false gods of this world.

Their idols are silver and gold, made by human hands. ⁵They have mouths, but cannot speak, eyes, but cannot see. ⁶They have ears, but cannot hear, noses, but cannot smell. ⁷They have hands, but cannot feel, feet, but cannot walk. They cannot make a sound with their throats. ⁸Those who make them are just like them, as are all who trust in them. Psalm 115:4-8

Our Sovereign, All-powerful, Creator God who loves us with the love of a Father and who has a throne in the heavenly places, lives within me and He is accomplishing all that pleases Him in and through my life. I have heard it said that the Christian's life should be the most confusing thing ever to a non-believer. It should defy the logic of the natural man. A Christian's life will be marked by peace even in the midst of terrible circumstances because they can rest with confidence as their Father leads them.

This was true of the disciple's lives; they knew what they believed about God and they believed what they knew. It made a difference in their lives. They didn't throw away their faith in God when trials came. They didn't listen to the voice of the accuser who told them that God had somehow failed to be faithful to them. Instead, they believed what they knew to be true about God and they acted on the things they knew to be true.

Finally brothers, whatever is true, whatever is honorable, whatever is just, whatever is pure, whatever is lovely, whatever is commendable—if there is any moral excellence and if there is any praise—dwell on these things. ⁹*Do what you have learned and received and heard and seen in me*, and the God of peace will be with you. Philippians 4:8-9 (emphasis added)

Know what you believe and believe what you know! Do it.

This is what I know: He is a faithful, loving, all-powerful God, who loves me with an everlasting, faithful love of a Father and He will never leave me.

Because I know this to be true, I believe it, and my life actions and my attitudes will be lived around those truths. I may not understand the ways of God, and I may not have eyes to see the good or know how I will ever make it through the Valley of Tears, but I will filter my thoughts and my actions around the truths that I know about God. I will find rest in these truths, a peace in my heart that surpasses the understanding of those around me. When others see me, they will see my God and know what I believe about Him.

For a child will be born for us, a son will be given to us, and the government will be on His shoulders. He will be named Wonderful Counselor, Mighty God, Eternal Father, Prince of Peace. Isaiah 9:6

My prayer is that each person walking through the Valley of Tears would learn to listen to the voice of the One who loves them, reach for his hand and walk on. May they find their source of strength to be the spring water that can only come from the presence of God Himself.

Jesus said, "Everyone who drinks from this water will get thirsty again. ¹⁴But whoever drinks from the water that I will give him will never get thirsty again—ever! In fact, the water I will give him will become a well of water springing up within him for eternal life." John 4:13-14

Happy are the people whose strength is in You, whose hearts are set on pilgrimage. ⁶As they pass through the Valley of Tears, they make it a source of springwater; even the autumn rain will cover it with blessings. ⁷They go from strength to strength; each appears before God in Zion. Psalm 84:5-7

Just between you and me, God: _____
_____
_____
_____
_____
_____

The Blessing

Week 2

The Refining Valley of Transformation – Because He Promised

Happy are the people whose strength is in You, whose hearts are set on pilgrimage. ⁶As they pass through the Valley of Tears, they make it a source of springwater; even the autumn rain will cover it with blessings. ⁷They go from strength to strength; each appears before God in Zion. Psalm 84:5-7

We have spent a week discovering what we know about God and assimilating those truths into beliefs that govern our lives. We know with certainty that God is mighty and trustworthy and we have understood that God will be the source of our strength as we travel through this valley of tears.

But as I read these verses, I am still a little mystified by the reference to joy; to the valley becoming a source of springwater;, and the reference to the blessing of autumn rains. How can anything that is connected to this valley of tears be considered a blessing? How can we find renewal and joy in a valley place? It seems contradictory. On the surface, we only see the hardship, but if we look into God's word at the examples of people and nations who have walked through dark valleys, we will discover what God was doing in their lives. As you know, one of the most common questions people have when they are suffering is "Why?" Although God has never promised to answer that question, we have many examples in the Bible which illustrate some reasons for suffering. As we look at these situations and see the work that God was accomplishing in their lives and in the lives of others, we will discover the choice fruit of blessing that lies beneath that bitter outer peel.

When we accepted Christ as our Savior, we became a new creation.

Therefore if anyone is in Christ, there is a new creation; old things have passed away, and look, new things have come. II Corinthians 5:17

This is actually a promise from God of great hope because He is not content to leave us as we are. We are no longer children of the darkness, we are children of His, and He has promised to make us new.

Ephesians 2:1-5 describes our condition as having been dead in our trespasses and sins, but now we are made alive with Christ! This means we are in for a transformation. He wants to remove our old, sinful dead way of living so that we can experience the newness of life.

I heard a father, Scott Phillips, describe the heart-wrenching experience of taking his two-year-old son to the hospital for surgery to determine if the lump that had grown on the boy's hand was cancerous or not. The boy was terrified to be laid on the hospital bed and to be surrounded by people he didn't know, and his eyes filled with tears as he begged with out-stretched arms for his dad to pick him up and take him away. The dad described that moment as one of the hardest moments in his life. Everything in him wanted to pick the boy up, hug him and walk out of the hospital, but he knew that he couldn't, and he knew that it was because of his decision as a father that the boy was in there in the first place. He also knew that in a few minutes the hand of his precious little boy would be cut open with a scalpel and the lump removed for biopsy. However scary and painful this situation was for his son, the dad knew that it was necessary for his son's life. This painful procedure would remove something from the boy that had the potential of destroying his life later on.

The father's decision was excruciating because he loved his son deeply, but in the end, he allowed the boy to experience the painful surgery because it was what the boy needed to live.

Scott later spoke about this event and said that he learned a lot about the love of our heavenly Father through that experience. He understood that God, as our Father, will not allow us to endure the pain of suffering unless there is something of great worth to be gained at the end of the experience. A Father simply loves us too much to allow suffering and pain for no purpose.

Ladies, one of the blessings that can come in our lives as a result of God leading us through a valley of tears is that God will do a work of refinement in our lives. He will be revealing to us the things that are still a part of our old life, things that keep others from seeing Him when they look at us. You are probably all familiar with the process of refining precious metals. In that process, minerals that have been deemed of value are subjected to extreme temperatures which cause the impurities to separate from the valued metals so the refiner can skim the dross, or the impurities, away. At the end of the process, the metal is purer and of greater value. Ladies, when we experience the refining hand of God in our lives, we can gratefully accept the purifying work as a blessing from the hand of God. Remember as our Father, God loves us too much to allow us to suffer without something of great value to be gained and a journey through a valley of refinement is for our transformation.

Do not be conformed to this age, but be transformed by the renewing of your mind, so that you may discern what is the good, pleasing, and perfect will of God. Romans 12:2

Ladies, embrace the thought that God is doing an internal work in us. He wants to renew us from the inside out, removing all that is left of the dead life and replacing it with abundant life. He has a goal of making us more like Himself. He wants us to know what He is like. He wants to introduce Himself to us, not merely as poetic words on the pages of our Bible, but in a real and tangible way. He is alive, and He wants us to feel His breath on our necks as He speaks to us. He wants us to realize and know that He is our greatest treasure. He wants us to know Him so well that we will follow Him wherever He leads us.

What can keep us from knowing Him in this passionate way?

Jesus warned in Matthew 13:15-16, and again in Revelation 3:14-22 about people who hear, but don't hear. People who see with their eyes, and yet do not see. Jesus is talking about complacency.

Another place that we see people who are no longer passionate about God is in the book of Malachi. The prophet, Malachi is delivering a message from God which will be the last message the nation of Israel receives from Him for 400 years. God was about to send a famine of his words to His people. What was happening in the lives of the Israelites at that time which would cause God to respond this way? What was the spiritual temperature at the time that Malachi came and delivered this message from God?

God declared His covenant of everlasting love toward His people in chapter 1, and they responded to His declaration with a question, "How did you love us?" God had chosen the descendants of Jacob to be His beloved nation of Israel. He had spoken to them, given them His laws and pledged Himself to them. He had blessed them in ways that He had not blessed the other nations. He had given Himself to this nation of Israel to be their God, yet they doubted His love.

- They had eyes to see, but they didn't see. They didn't even believe what they knew was true.

We also learn in chapter 1 they were giving offerings to the Lord as required, but they were withholding their best lambs and giving God their diseased animals. They didn't want to give their best to the Lord, so they offered Him their leftovers.

- They had eyes to see, but they didn't see. They refused to honor God with their best.

We discover in chapter two, that the religious leaders were not honoring God either. They were watering down the messages from God and confusing people instead of being clear messengers for God.

- They had ears to hear, but they didn't hear. They were not leading others to God with their words.

Marriage vows were not being regarded in high honor and men were abandoning their spouses. God reminded the nation that they were to be faithful and to produce Godly offspring!

- They had ears to hear, but they didn't hear. They were not people of their word. Vows were not binding. Convenience and pleasure ruled.

In chapters 1-2, God's people accused Him of being unfair. Their cold hearts didn't understand why God was upset with the way they were living. They were content to live mediocre lives, half following God and half like the world around them. I am sure when they told God that He was unjust and demanded to much from them, that they hoped He would just leave them alone. Instead, God answered their accusation with a promise that He would be sending someone soon who would refine them as a nation.

But who can endure the day of His coming? And who will be able to stand when He appears? For He will be like a refiner's fire and like cleansing lye. ³He will be like a refiner and purifier of silver; He will purify the sons of Levi and refine them like gold and silver. Then they will present offerings to the LORD in righteousness. Malachi 3:2-3

God had chosen the nation of Israel to be His representative here on earth. As this nation lived by God's laws, the surrounding Gentile nations would be introduced to God. This was a unique relationship God had ordained with Israel. He had pledged Himself to be their God and they had promised to be His people. God would make them a great nation; for the long-awaited Messiah would come from them, and the entire world would be blessed through them. But instead of living up to the high calling that they had been given, they instead chose to embrace the things of the world. They were content to live like the other nations who didn't know God. They wanted to do all the things that the world was doing. They had grown complacent, satisfied with themselves, no longer looking and seeking after the things of God. They had eyes to see, but they did not see. They had ears to hear, but they did not hear.

This was not a nation of people living in outright rebellion; they were full of religious activity, but their duty-oriented hearts had stolen God's honor. Their half-hearted obedience robbed them of the abundant life that God wanted them to live. Instead of worshipping the giver of their gifts, they had begun to worship and crave the gifts.

God's desire for holiness was in their best interest. They were the ones missing out on all that they could experience in life because they had grown content to play in the "mud puddle" when God had offered them a "beach-front house." They would need a wake-up call from God, and God was about to lead them into a dark valley of refinement. He would be silent before them. They would not hear any new words from Him. He wasn't abandoning them, but this sudden silence would be deafening, and it should have sent them running to Him. So how did Israel respond when they found themselves in that dark valley place? Did they seek Him? Did they turn to Him or did create their own form of "hearing" from God by writing religious laws of their own?

Can you understand how much more God wanted for this nation? He had chosen them, but they had grown apathetic toward Him; they had become content and comfortable with the way things were, and it was because God knew what they were missing that he prepared a valley of refinement for them. He gave the nation the opportunity to be purified so that they could be all that He had planned for them.

In the fullness of time, 400 years later, God sent His son, Jesus, to this world. He came as the **Word** of God in the flesh! God wouldn't send a messenger to deliver His words anymore, He came himself clothed in human flesh.

Eleven men, whose hearts had been prepared through the refining process, were tucked away in the hills and valleys of Galilee. They were waiting for the promised Messiah, and when they met Jesus, they followed Him straightway! At that time, the nation as a whole missed what God had planned for them (but God is not finished with Israel, and the refining process is still happening). Within the nation, when Jesus came, there were individuals whose hearts had been made ready, and they eagerly received the life that God desired for them. They had eyes to see and ears to hear.

What about us? Are we guilty of seeing, but not seeing; of hearing, but not hearing? Do we grow blind and deaf and just accept the status quo? Have you ever found yourself content with the way things are in your life? Do we "believe" things about God, but don't live like we "believe" them? We may have grown satisfied with where we are in our lives, but God sees a more significant picture, and he is not content to leave us the way we are; remember, He is in the transformation business!

C. S. Lewis once said, "Imagine yourself as a living house. God comes in to rebuild that house. At first, perhaps, you can understand what He is doing. He is getting the drains right and stopping the leaks in the roof and so on; you knew that those jobs needed doing and so you are not surprised. But presently He starts knocking the house about in a way that hurts abominably and does not seem to make any sense… What on earth is He up to? The explanation is that He is building quite a different house from the one you thought of—throwing out a new wing here, putting on an extra floor there, running up towers, making courtyards. You thought you were being made into a decent little cottage: but he is building a palace. He intends to come and live there Himself."[1]

We are not often aware of all that God wants to accomplish through us because we are usually blind to how much of the dead-life needs to be rooted out of us because we have grown accustomed to it.

One morning I discovered that the neighborhood herd of wild pigs had visited my yard in the night. The piles of leaves that I had just raked were spread from one side of the yard to the other, and there were holes and trenches everywhere. To say I wasn't thrilled would be an understatement. I hadn't planned

---

[1] Lewis, C.S. *Mere Christianity* (Macmillan Publishers, U.S. 1952)

to invest any more time than necessary to rake up those leaf piles. The mess in my yard would require a lot more time and energy than I had planned to invest in it.

I began to work in my yard with the simplest intention of just smoothing out the ruts from the pigs and raking the leaves back into piles. But as soon as I started to rake the leaves and fill in holes, I noticed some branches that needed to be picked up and a few Palmetto bushes that needed to be trimmed. There were also vines and Spanish moss that should be pulled down along with tree limbs that could be pruned. The more time I spent out there, the more things I noticed that required my attention. When we had moved there three years before, it was just a semi-wooded area in the middle of our circular drive. It was overgrown, and I hadn't paid much attention to it. I had grown accustomed to the way it looked. It wasn't until I was out there cleaning up the mess that the pigs had made that I started to get a vision for how pretty that section of the yard could look. I trimmed the trees and cut the scrubby growth; my husband helped and we planted grass. I hung up some potted flowers, and for the first time, our front yard was starting to look good.

It took weeks to restore order to the mess that the pigs made. Since then, my grass has grown in nicely, and I am dreaming about some wicker furniture and some white lights in the trees! But it was only after the pigs came that I began to look with eyes to see, and began to notice all the things that needed attention.

We can be like the Israelites, content with the status quo. God is not content with the status quo. Because He loves us, He sees the areas in our lives that still need to be transformed, and He will lovingly allow us to endure the heat of the refinery. It is during this process that the dross, the things that have cluttered our hearts' affections, are removed, and we begin to experience the abundant life of living our lives wholeheartedly for God.

One blessing of the valley is that we are reintroduced to God, for He is truly our greatest treasure. The Valley stirs things up in our lives so that we begin to see with eyes that see, and we let go of all the things that we have collected in our lives that have kept us from knowing the abundant life that God has planned for us.

It is because of His great love for us; He is not content to let us stay conformed to the world. He wants us to know the good and pleasing will of God! He wants us to enjoy the privilege of living a life that accomplishes much for Him.

In our homework lessons this week, we will look at some examples of great leaders of God who endured deep trials of the soul, who walked through the Valley of Tears, but in the end, emerged purified and strengthened to accomplish great works for God!

For God, who said, "Light shall shine out of darkness" —He has shone in our hearts to give the light of the knowledge of God's glory in the face of Jesus Christ. ⁷Now we have this treasure in clay jars, so that this extraordinary power may be from God and not from us. ⁸We are pressured in every way but not crushed; we are perplexed but not in despair; ⁹we are persecuted but not abandoned; we are struck down but not destroyed. ¹⁰We always carry the death of Jesus in our body, so that the life of Jesus may also be revealed in our body. II Corinthians 4:6-10

God is at work in our lives, carefully tending to us. At times it may seem like we cannot survive, but His hand will never allow the temperature to get any hotter than what is needed for our purification.

Yet He knows the way I have taken; when He has tested me, I will emerge as pure gold. Job 23:10

The Refiner's Fire

He sat by a furnace of seven-fold heat,
As He watched by the precious ore.
And closer He bent with a searching gaze,
As He heated it more and more.

He knew He had ore that could stand the test
And He wanted the finest gold,
To mold as a crown, for the king to wear,
Set with gems of price untold.

So He laid our gold in the burning fire,
Tho' we fain would say Him "nay."
And watched the dross that we had not seen
As it melted and passed away.

And the gold grew brighter and got more bright,
But our eyes were dim with tears,
We saw but the fire, not the Master's hand,
And questioned with anxious fears.

Yet our gold shone out with a richer glow
As it mirrored a form above,
That bent o'er the fire, though unseen by us
With a look of ineffable love.

Can we think it pleases His loving heart
To cause us moments of pain?
Ah, no! But He sees through the present cross
The bliss of eternal gain.

So He waited there with a watchful eye,
With a love that is strong and sure.
And His gold did not suffer a bit more heat
Than was needed to make it pure.

Author - **A.F. Ingler**

The Blessing

Day 1

God's Vision for Us

I am sure of this, that He who started a good work in you will carry it on to completion until the day of Christ Jesus. Philippians 1:6

I love this verse. God has started a work in you and me, and he will carry it out until it is completed! II Corinthians 5:17 tells us that we are a new creation in Christ. He is at work creating something new in us! I am sure you have heard of Michelangelo, the great Italian sculptor, and painter of the 1400s-1500s, who in 1504 completed his most famous work, the sculpture of David. Another sculptor had begun the job, but Michelangelo finished it. He claimed that he could see the finished piece when he looked at the block of marble. He created the finished product by chipping away all of the stone that didn't belong in the finished work. I heard someone remark that you rarely hear the name of that sculpture without it being paired with the name of the sculptor: "Michelangelo's David." The person went on to say that we should be known as: "God's Jodie," or "God's _____." You can put your name or the name of a loved one in the blank. We are His workmanship, and He will continue the work until it is completed!

Write out II Corinthians 3:18. _____
_____

When we spend time in God's word, James tells us that it is like looking into a mirror. The Bible says that as new creatures in Christ, we are being transformed into His image so we can be quite confident that He is carving away all the characteristics and qualities in our lives that do not reflect his glory. Therefore, we should not be surprised at the "chipping" process.

Write out I Corinthians 13:12. _____
_____

We don't see or understand it all clearly right now. We know only the moment. We don't have the transcendent quality that God does to see the whole picture. He considers the generations before and the generations that follow, and he completes a work in us that is creating a reflection of His glory. This process of transformation takes time. He sees us for what we can be, and the work that can be accomplished through us to show His exceeding greatness to others and He begins the process of conforming us to his image.

As we explore examples in Scripture of men and women whom God used to accomplish works for Him, we note that they are celebrated because they trusted God by being faithful to Him in the midst of great difficulty. God doesn't ask men and women to do the easy things. That would come naturally to us; it is easy to love those who love us, but God asks us to love our enemies! He asks us to go beyond what is natural to us and trust Him by doing the hard thing. We are not asked to live our lives by sight, but to live them by faith in Him.

Consider Abraham, a man who one day was living life as regularly as he ever had and then the next day, he had an encounter with God which changed his life completely!

Genesis 12:1-3 The LORD had said to Abram: "_____
²I will make you into a great nation, I will bless you, I will make your name great, and you will be a blessing. ³I will bless those who bless you, I will curse those who treat you with contempt, and all the peoples on earth will be blessed through you." ⁴ _____
_____ and Lot went with him. Abram was 75 years old when he left Haran.**

Abraham was being asked to leave everything he knew to go someplace that God would tell him later. Imagine trying to explain that to his wife! They packed up and said goodbye to their friends and family and began a journey to an unknown place. They had to trust in an unseen God to lead them down a road they had never traveled before, and they had no idea where it would end.

Have you ever felt like God was asking you to trust him on an unknown path? _____
_____
_____

We feel more comfortable when we know the way that we are taking. We are at ease driving to and from our local hangouts. We know the way; we know what to expect and are not surprised or uncomfortable along the way. It is different when you strike out on the road and can't see where it goes or know what to expect. The security in all of this is that God promises to go with us. We are never alone on the unknown roads! He is with us. We can talk to Him. His presence gives us peace.

Abraham is also promised that he will have a son and that God will make a great nation from that son. At age 99, God still had not fulfilled that promise. Abraham had to wait for a long time for God to fulfill the promise of a son. The waiting time was also a time of testing, a time to prove to Abraham that as God, He could be trusted to fulfill His word, even when if it seemed like He had forgotten.

Have you ever felt like God was never going to answer a prayer? _____
_____
_____

I know people who prayed for the salvation of a loved one for over 50 years before God answered their heart-felt prayer!

Abraham didn't pass the waiting test very well. He grew anxious and manipulated a way for a son to be born through his wife's maidservant. This was not the promised son, and that decision to act in a way outside of God's promise would bear grave consequences through the ages. It wasn't until Abraham was 100 years old that God fulfilled his promise and gave him Isaac.

I am sure that Abraham was happy and probably thought that his troubles were finally over. He was in the land where God had led him, and he finally had the promised son; God's promise of making a great nation from his offspring could now be fulfilled! What a glorious day!

But in a few years, God had one more test for Abraham. This would prove to be the most difficult trial of all. God asked Abraham to take Isaac to Mount Moriah, to prepare an altar and to sacrifice his son upon that altar.

Read Genesis 22.

The Blessing

Abraham trusted God enough to offer the most precious thing he had to God. He was willing to sacrifice his son because God had asked him to (imagine the sorrow and the pain of that decision!). In God's kind providence, he spared the life of Isaac after Abraham demonstrated that His heart was willing to give it all up for God.

God was refining a life. He was chiseling away at the character of Abraham and putting him in places of intense trial so that the character of God could be proven to be faithful and Abraham's faith in God would grow. Abraham was be willing to trust God, and obey Him as he was being fashioned into the image of the one who created and loved Him.

God, who could see the beginning from the end, knew what Abraham needed to learn about Him and prepared the way so that Abraham could learn and become the man that God wanted him to become.

Abraham is remembered by God in Hebrews, chapter 11, which is often called God's "Hall of Faith." God celebrates the lives of people who believed Him and lived extraordinary lives.

Read Hebrews 11:8-19. Write out some of the wonderful things that God says in his description of Abraham's life. _____
_____
_____

Was Abraham's life comfortable? Did he endure great times of difficulty and trial? Do you think Abraham ever cried? I am sure that he did, but in all that he lived through, he chose to believe and trust God, and God counted that as righteousness!

What about you? Can you trust God? Can you believe that God sees beyond the moment and is creating something of infinitely greater value in your life and in the lives of those you love? Can you believe Him for the big picture? Will you be faithful in your trial?

Just between you and me, God: _____
_____
_____
_____
_____

Day 2

The Favored One

Now Israel loved Joseph more than his other sons because Joseph was a son born to him in his old age, and he made a robe of many colors for him. Genesis 37:3

In a perfect world, this would never happen - one child favored over the others. But we know that sometimes, as in the case of Joseph, Jacob's heart was drawn to favor this son because he had been born in Jacob's later years. Whatever the reason may be, favoring one child over another will set the family up for a lifetime of conflict.

This was the case in the family of Joseph. Genesis chapters 37-50 tell the story of Joseph's life. Joseph was the 11th son of Jacob and his most cherished son. Joseph's mom, Rachel, was also the beloved wife. Joseph's life is a testimony of a man who endured countless injustices, yet forgave the ones who wronged him, because he recognized that God's hand was guiding his life.

God would transplant young Joseph out of his home country and place him as a slave and a prisoner in the foreign land of Egypt so that Joseph could be used as the deliverer for his family when a severe famine came upon their land. God had chosen Joseph. He was a favored one (God has also chosen us, and we too are also his favored ones!). But, before this chosen one would be ready to complete the task that God had for him, Joseph needed to experience a season of refinement. Joseph would lose self-confidence and learn God-confidence.

Let's look at Joseph's growing up years.

Jacob didn't hide the fact that he favored Joseph and commissioned a unique, colorful jacket to be made for Joseph (Genesis 37:3). Imagine for a few minutes what it might have been like to grow up in a home with a favored brother.

Now envision for a moment what Joseph might have felt like growing up as the favored one? Do you think he got special privileges? Was he exempt from certain less-desirable chores? Do you think he got to sit in "the front seat" more often? Was it possible that he began to think he was pretty special?

I picture Joseph growing up with constant positive affirmation. In his dad's eye, there probably wasn't a thing he could do wrong. I am guessing that in front of Jacob, even the brothers had to at least act like they liked Joseph. I think Joseph grew up like a lot of kids do today, with the world revolving around them. He had a pretty good life until he was about 17, then things started to change.

In Genesis 37:2, we learn that when Joseph was 17, he was tending the sheep with his brothers and when he got home he tattled to his dad about something they had done. We don't have any idea what their offense was; it may have had to do with the way they were taking care of the sheep, but I have a suspicion that it might have had more to do with something they said or did to Joseph.

How did Joseph's brothers feel about him according to Genesis 37:4?_____

It didn't help matters when Joseph decided to tell his brothers about the dreams he'd had where they were bowing down to him. By the time we get to verses 12-32, the brothers had decided to sell Joseph to a band of traveling merchants who were on their way to Egypt. The brothers concealed their treachery from their father by taking Joseph's coat, dipping it into the blood of an animal, and lying about finding it in the wilderness. Jacob was, of course, heartbroken and he refused to be comforted by anyone.

Meanwhile, Joseph was sold as a slave to a high-ranking ruler in Egypt. He served as a personal servant to Potiphar. Read Genesis 39:1-6 and describe what Joseph's life was like as a slave in Potiphar's household. _____
_____

I love that even in this awful situation, as a slave in a foreign land, separated from his loving father; the LORD was with Joseph and prospered him. That is such an encouragement to my heart. When things seem like they can't get any worse, God is with me, and He can help me to do well in any situation.

The Blessing

One of Joseph's hardest trials happens in Genesis 39:7-20. Why was Joseph thrown into prison? Had he done anything wrong? _____
_____

Describe the kinds of emotions you think Joseph might have been feeling? _____
_____

I remember one of the most painful emotional experiences that I've had in recent years came at a time when I thought I was doing a particular task well, and helping someone. They misunderstood my intentions and instead of being happy with my help were angry at me. It was a shocking blow. It was hurtful and confusing. It sent me to my knees. For a long time, in my disappointment and shock, I focused on the pain and listened to the voice that told me how unfair the situation was. I sat in my puddle of tears for a long time. I forgot to believe what I knew to be true about God: that He is sovereign and all-powerful, that He loves me with the unfailing love of a father, that He will never leave me, and that His presence brings peace and comfort to me.

My loving Heavenly Father comforted my wounded heart at that time. I think when we do something wrong, we expect a chastisement to come, not that we enjoy it, but we understand it and are not surprised by it. But when we are handed a trial instead of the blessing we expected, it can knock the wind out of us, and we stagger at the surprise.

Joseph went to prison, but what does Genesis 39:21 say? _____
_____

Even here in this great time of disappointment, the LORD had not left Joseph! He granted him favor in the eyes of the warden and Joseph was promoted to a supervisor of the prisoners. God was blessing everything that Joseph did. He was still in prison, but God's hand was guiding Joseph.

When Joseph is given the ability to interpret a couple dreams of fellow prisoners, one prisoner promises to say a good word on Joseph's behalf to the Pharaoh when he got out of prison.

What does Genesis 40:23 say happened? _____

How much time passed? Genesis 41:1 _____

Joseph may have felt his lowest during those two years. He might have wondered why God had allowed these awful events in his life. This life wasn't anything like what he had dreamed it would be. Surely it felt like God had made a colossal mistake with his life. What good had come of all of Joseph's efforts to do the right things? What reward did he get? Hated by his family, sold as a slave, imprisoned for years because of a false accusation and then forgotten by someone who said he would help him. We don't know what Joseph thought or felt during those years, but we do know that eventually Pharaoh had some dreams and Joseph was called out of prison to interpret the dreams. God gave Joseph the wisdom to understand their meaning and the Pharaoh was pleased with Joseph and promoted him to the second in command of all of Egypt! Wow! That must have been a shock to Joseph's system! He had thought he was forgotten and then the next thing he knows, he's second in command of all of Egypt!

God's plan for Joseph wasn't over yet, but Joseph had now been prepared for the work that God had sent Joseph to do in Egypt. God would reunite Joseph with his brothers and Joseph would have a heart that would extend grace and forgiveness. The old Joseph, who believed his own press, had been stripped of pride and the confidence that had been built into his life by all the favor that he had received from his father, Jacob. The new Joseph had learned to trust God, not himself. The new Joseph had learned how to forgive others and not let the seed of bitterness grow in his heart. He had learned that God was working behind the scenes in ways that he couldn't understand, and when the time came for Jacob's family to find refuge in Egypt, they would find Joseph, the man whom God had refined. They would find safety and provision because God had prepared the way for them through the refinement of Joseph.

But Joseph said to them, "Don't be afraid. Am I in the place of God? [20]You planned evil against me; God planned it for good to bring about the present result—the survival of many people. [21]Therefore don't be afraid. I will take care of you and your little ones." And he comforted them and spoke kindly to them. Genesis 50:19-21

Just between you and me, God: _____
_____
_____
_____
_____
_____

Day 3

A Meek Spirit

Now the man Moses was very meek, above all the men which were upon the face of the earth. Numbers 12:3 (KJV)

If we were asked to describe a modern day hero we might choose words like, strong, protective, confident, brave, faithful, etc. I'm not sure many of us would choose the word "meek." It has a weak sound to it, and we generally prefer words of strength or power to describe our heroes.

Except for the fact that meek and weak rhyme, they have nothing else in common. The word meek simply means humble. Instead of being filled with high notions about themselves, a meek person recognizes that their true source of power and strength come from God. God is looking for people who are willing to yield themselves to Him so that He can fill them and produce a life that is characterized by the strength and power of God! This is far more impressive in a hero than someone who puffs himself up and labors in his own strength.

How is it that this character trait came to be used to describe Moses?

Take a few moments and read Exodus chapters 1-3. It only takes a few minutes to read, but these chapters cover 80 years of Moses' life! God had a great plan for Moses and it included leading a nation of around two million people out of the land of Egypt away from a powerful Pharaoh. Moses would lead these people through a barren desert for forty years. It wouldn't be an easy task, but God's hand

The Blessing

had been working purposefully in Moses' life from his first breath, preparing him for the work that God had planned for him to accomplish.

Moses' first 40 years were spent growing up in the nation of Egypt. He was a Hebrew, and the Hebrews were slaves to the Egyptians. Moses' parents were slaves; they were forced to work long hard hours and were denied personal rights. In Exodus 1:16, what were the midwives commanded to do if a Hebrew slave woman gave birth to a baby boy? _____

Apparently, the rulers in Egypt ruled without compassion for their slaves or their families.

In chapter 2, we learn that Moses' mother, Jochebed, tried to hide baby Moses for three months, but we all know that as babies get older and bigger, their cries get louder and their waking times longer. When it became impossible for Jochebed, to hide him any longer, she prepared a basket of reeds for her baby. She waterproofed the basket with pitch and tar and carefully laid her son in the basket and set him adrift in the Nile River. Because we are familiar with the story and even know the ending, we are often guilty of not feeling the emotions that would have overwhelmed this poor mother.

We know that Moses was rescued by an Egyptian princess and that Moses was raised in the palace by the Pharaohs' daughter making him a grandson to the ruling Pharaoh.

There's not a lot of information about Moses during these years. We know that he lived in Egypt for the first 40 years of his life. We assume that he spent a large part of his days receiving instruction in academic subjects, as well as the art of war. He would have been taught the religious system of the Egyptians. Moses did know that he had been born a Hebrew and he knew who his family was.

We have no way of knowing, but I wonder if Moses was able to visit with his family on occasion? We know that the princess allowed him to live with his family until he was old enough to be weaned. After that, we don't know if he had a relationship with his family, but I like to think that he did have some contact with them, and I think it was during these brief visitations that Moses' parents taught him about the one true God of their fathers. I think he had been taught about God's promise to Abraham, Isaac, and Jacob. Certainly, Moses knew about his ancestors because when he left Egypt, they carried Joseph's bones with them.

Imagine how difficult this life was for Moses' family. It would be like having Child Protective Services show up at your door without any just cause and demanding your three-month-old boy, and then only allowing you visitation rights on occasion. This was a dark valley of tears for Moses and his mother.

Yet, God would use this horribly dark and frightful time in Moses' life to begin to prepare him for the future role of leader. Had Moses not been chosen to walk through that valley place, he would have lived at home with his family as a slave. He would never have received the training that he needed to rescue the Israelites from Egypt. Moses hadn't been given a "heads up" to God's plan; he didn't have any idea that this valley of tears would equip him to complete a marvelous task that God had prepared for him.

During those first 40 years of Moses' life, he learned the necessary skills to govern people, but I think his confidence was rooted in himself. In Exodus 2:11-12, we start to get a little insight into what Moses' heart was like at this point in his life.

Write out both verses. _____
_____

_____
_____
_____
_____
_____
_____

Moses recognized the hardship that his fellow people were enduring, and he was enraged that they were being treated so terribly.

Verse 12 tells us that Moses looked around to make sure no one was looking and then he killed the Egyptian who had beaten the Hebrew. Taking the life of someone is a horrific act of violence. Moses didn't accidentally kill the man, he looked around before he did it to make sure he didn't get caught. Maybe you are tempted to think of Moses as an action hero coming to the rescue of the Hebrew people, but Moses acted in his own strength, confident in himself, his authority and his position. He had an independent and proud spirit, and that kind of spirit always acts outside the power of God.

Pharaoh did find out about the murder and wanted to execute Moses for the crime. Moses had to run. This was another dark valley in Moses' life. He literally had to run for his life! He left behind everything he had ever known. He escaped and ended up in the desert area of Midian. Mind you, he was a cultured, pampered prince! He went from having everything he needed with servants to help him, to absolute, abject poverty, sitting on the side of a well dug in the desert. While he was sitting there, he met a woman who invited him to her father's house, and eventually, Moses married one of this man's daughters.

Moses, "the prince," would spend the next 40 years of his life living like a nomadic shepherd tending a flock of sheep in the wilderness. Egyptians hated shepherds, believing them to be a low class of people. Being a shepherd would have been a humbling experience for Moses. Daily, Moses would lead a flock of sheep, search for food and water, while guiding and protecting them. He would spend many lonely days and nights in the wilderness. He would spend much time alone, probably rethinking his life and the emptiness of position and prestige. It is all as a vapor, here for a moment and gone. What's left is the reality that we only have God and that God is enough for our need! Only God gives purpose and meaning to our lives. In those 40 years spent in the desert, Moses had the time and the opportunity to be refined into a man who depended on God, a man who found his strength and purpose in God.

In chapter 3, we read about God appearing to Moses in that desert place and speaking to him out of a burning bush. God instructed Moses to return to Egypt and rescue the Hebrew people.

Read Exodus chapter 4. Moses had three excuses for not wanting to go back to Egypt, what were they?

Exodus 4:1 _____

Exodus 4:10 _____

Exodus 4:13 _____

I believe that Moses understood that **he** had nothing to offer by way of authority, power or knowledge. Moses' excuses were born out of a humble heart, empty of self-pretense. He had learned the lessons that God had been teaching him during his time in the desert. It would only be through God infusing Moses with authority, power, and knowledge, that Moses would be effective in the work that God had planned for him. God assured Moses that he would go in the authority of Jehovah God, empowered to do miraculous things by God's power, and the very presence of God would be speaking through him.

Moses went and did as the Lord commanded. We don't have time in this lesson to talk about the rest of Moses' life, but from what we have studied, we know that he did not have a comfortable life. He experienced many trials and hardships, but in those dark valley times in his life, God was preparing Moses for the marvelous purpose that God had planned for him.

Moses spent 40 years in the wilderness, learning to let go of his self-confidence and learning to depend on God. When we learn to yield ourselves to God and allow Him to work through us, we develop the spirit of meekness, and we operate with the supernatural power of God.

God, who sees the beginning from the end, had chosen Moses for the work of redeeming the Hebrew people from Egypt. He began a refining process in Moses' life, preparing him for the tasks that He had planned for him to do.

Moses didn't see the big picture, he only saw the moment, just like you and I. Moses stayed moldable and willingly endured the refining fires to be fashioned into the meek leader who would yield his life to God and complete the works that God had planned for him to do!

Write out Exodus 33:11a. _____
_____

A meek man, yielded to God, was called a friend of God!

Blessed are the gentle: because they will inherit the earth. Matthew 5:5

Just between you and me, God: _____
_____
_____
_____
_____

Happy are the people whose strength is in You, whose hearts are set on pilgrimage. ⁶As they pass through the Valley of Tears, they make it a source of springwater; even the autumn rain will cover it will blessings. ⁷They go from strength to strength; each appears before God in Zion. Psalm 84:5-7

Day 4

The Giver or the Gift?

LORD, You are my portion and my cup of blessing; You hold my future. Psalm 16:5

We saw in the life of Abraham a severe test in which God asked Abraham to sacrifice the most important thing in his life. God was testing Abraham to see his heart. Would Abraham cling tightly to the gift that God had given him or would he hold that gift with open hands and offer that gift back to God?

God blesses us with many gifts, and we sometimes let the abundance of gifts overshadow the giver. We can develop a greater love for the gift than the giver of the gift. In the refining process of our lives, God may take us through a valley where He strips us of the things we believe we cannot live without, to show us His incomparable worth. For our own benefit, he refocuses our hearts on the one thing that truly satisfies: the Giver, himself! I have heard it said that when we get to the place where all we have is God, we will discover that He is all we need.

When I think of people in the Bible who were brought through great trials by God to refine them for His higher purpose, I think of the shepherd boy David. David was the youngest son in a family of eight boys. From I Samuel, chapter 16, we know that his family hadn't any great hope of David growing up to be a leader, much less the King of Israel. He was tending to the sheep and wasn't even called in to meet the prophet, Samuel. No one saw any great potential in him. God doesn't see us as we *are*, He sees us for what we *can* be!

God promised David that He would be the next King of Israel. I have loved studying David's life and watching his responses to the great trials that he endured on the path to Kingship. David never lost sight of God on that problematic journey; he didn't pursue the gift and forget about the giver. He loved God more than the promise of kingship, and I think that is one of the reasons that God described David as "a man after God's own heart."

After removing Saul, he made David their king. He testified concerning him: "I have found David son of Jesse a man after my own heart; he will do everything I want him to do." Acts 13:22 (NIV)

The HCSB translates that phrase "a man loyal to me." I like both translations because they show a heart with a singular purpose: God.

We first meet David in I Samuel, chapter 16. The prophet Samuel had been sent by God to the house of Jesse to anoint the man whom God had designated the next king of Israel.

When Samuel arrived at Jesse's home, he was introduced to the older sons. Samuel was impressed with the stature and strength of the oldest boy and felt confident that this would be the son that God would ask him to anoint. But according to I Samuel 16:7, what did God say to Samuel about that assumption?

_____
_____

What was God more interested in?_____

David's dad had not even requested him to come in and stand before the prophet, and when asked by Samuel if he had any other sons, Jesse responded, "The youngest, but he is tending the sheep." David was an unlikely choice by human understanding, but he was God's choice. David was summoned from the fields and was given a blessing by the prophet Samuel.

David was young when he was anointed by Samuel, and it wasn't until he was 30 years old that he was anointed king and assumed the throne over all of Israel. David probably waited 15-16 years from the time he was first anointed by Samuel until he took the throne.

The Blessing

II Samuel 5:1-4 records the anointing that took place when David assumed the throne of Israel. What does verse 2 say about what the Lord had made known to David? _____
_____

There wasn't any doubt in David's mind. He knew that God had told him that he would rule over Israel. This was a promise that God had made to David. This was a tremendous gift from God! Yet, David would experience about 15 years of waiting and great trials before that gift would actually be his. He wasn't given the details about how long he would have to wait; he lived in the moment, the same as you and I do. He knew that God had removed His blessing from King Saul and that he, David, was God's choice to be the next king.

King Saul was consumed with jealousy, and he pursued David relentlessly throughout those years. He sent armies to hunt down David and Saul himself joined in the pursuit several times. Saul wanted David killed. Not because David had done anything wrong, but because David was everything good!

Take a few moments and record some of the emotions that David might have felt running for his life from a crazed, jealous king. Think about the things that David had to give up while living on the run. Think about the things he might have thought about Saul. Put yourself in his place and write down some of the feelings that David might have experienced during this 15 year time period. _____
_____
_____

Two of my favorite stories about David are found in I Samuel 24 and in I Samuel 26. In both chapters, King Saul had been chasing David, and unbeknownst to Saul, he had gotten close enough to David where David had a clear opportunity to kill him. Each time David's servants encouraged David to kill the king. They told him that God had finally provided a way for David to assume the throne. Both times, David rejected their advice. In I Samuel 26:9-11, what did David tell his servant, Abishai? _____
_____
_____

These two accounts are remarkable to me. David would have been weary from years of running and had been deprived of living peacefully in Israel, the very nation that God had promised for him to rule. He hadn't been able to be with his family and friends enjoying his homeland for many years. He lived in caves and in foreign countries. Once, he had to pretend to be insane to preserve his life. He lived "roughing it" for more years than anyone would think were reasonable. But, when "given" the opportunity to kill Saul and end the trial, he refused to do so. David valued God over the promised gift of kingship. David trusted God for the timing of his gift. This was David's heart, not once, but twice. He trusted God and was willing to endure the journey through a dark, lonely valley of tears while he waited for God to fulfill His promise.

Trials are difficult, and sometimes we just want out of our valley of tears as quickly as possible. We can be tempted to take a shortcut out of there. Have you ever gotten tripped up on a test like this? Have you ever found yourself in this kind of situation? What did you do? Would you do the same thing again today if you had the chance to redo the test? _____
_____
_____
_____

I think of Abraham and Sarah when they were waiting for the promise of their son. As the years began to pass by, they grew impatient waiting, and they chose to take a shortcut, to "help" God out a little bit. They had Sarah's servant sleep with Abraham, and she conceived a child. Surely they had helped God out, and now they had their promised child, right? No, this was not the child that God had promised. God didn't need their help; as Creator God, He could choose to open Sarah's barren womb at the proper time. Abraham and Sarah's decision to take a shortcut out of their valley created the life of a little boy who would grow up with animosity towards Abraham's promised son and the conflict between the nations continues even to today.

About 15 years ago, I strongly felt the call to study the Bible in depth, and I had many opportunities to share the things that I had learned with women, and I felt fulfilled doing it. I was convinced that God had given a precious gift to me. In retrospect, I know that He had awakened my spirit and that the desire to teach was a gift from Him, but He had not offered that gift to me at that moment. He hadn't said, "This is what I want you to do *now*." His plan for me would include a trial of waiting and a time of refinement before I was ready for that gift. In my eagerness to have the gift, I grabbed it and pursued it, nurtured it and cherished it, for about three years, until God rather abruptly changed my path. He redirected my steps from my shortcut plan back to His primary plan for me; to teach and train my young family. This plan hadn't seemed as exciting to me. My kids didn't seem eager to learn from me! It was like a barren desert of repeatedly teaching the same things and correcting and admonishing wrong behaviors. God wanted to use those experiences to refine me and to refine my kids. I had mistakenly chosen to pursue the gift, excluding the Giver and His timing.

God spoke clearly to me, and I had a choice to make. I could obey God and step out of all the teaching roles to refocus on my family or hold tightly to this exciting gift of teaching and ignore the Giver. I obeyed God's voice in my heart, and I refocused on my precious children. God had not removed the gift of teaching from me; He just clearly showed me that I had not waited for his timing in it. He still had a lot of refining work to do in me. I hadn't quite finished all the assignments in my current chapter of life called, "Raising Your Children to Know and Love God." I am so glad that He is a God of forgiveness and redirection!

Write out Psalm 37:23. _____

_____

_____

A quick look through the Psalms penned by David shows us that David was a man of deep emotion. He experienced deep sorrow and great joy, but he brought all of those emotions to God in his prayers and songs and He allowed God to direct his steps, not his emotions! He was guided in his decisions by his love and trust in God! This may be one of the reasons that he is known as the man who had a heart like God!

Psalm 18, which is written by David after God delivered him from his enemies and from Saul, is one of my all-time favorite Psalms. Take a few minutes to read and meditate on it and then talk to God about your own trials.

The Blessing

Just between you and me, God: _____
_____
_____
_____
_____
_____
_____

I called to the LORD in my distress, and I cried to my God for help. From His temple, He heard my voice, and my cry to Him reached His ears. Psalm 18:6

Day 5

Highly Esteemed

He said, "Daniel, you who are highly esteemed…" Daniel 10:11a (NIV)

Do you remember in an earlier lesson when we said that God doesn't ask us to do easy things? Daniel is one of the men in the Bible who clearly illustrates this. Daniel is probably one of our favorite characters in the Bible because we are enamored with the story of God protecting him when he was thrown into a den of hungry lions. But may I suggest that this event was not an easy thing in Daniel's life? Daniel did not know the end of the story. We don't break out in a sweat reading the story because we know how it ends. Daniel wasn't given the ending of the story ahead of time. He was asked to live it out in real-time just as you and I are called to live our lives, trusting God at the moment, even in the hard moments. Daniel learned not to lean on his own understanding, but to trust God in the midst of every circumstance!

We have been talking about being led by God to the valley of tears for the purpose of refinement. God takes something that is precious to Him, us, and introduces it to the heat of a significant trial to reveal and skim away impurities, leaving behind a purer life which can be used for even greater purposes!

Read Daniel chapter 1.

When the Babylonian army invaded Judah and destroyed the city of Jerusalem, the king ordered the army to bring back some slaves. Who were they to bring back?

Daniel 1:3-4 _____
_____
_____

Daniel was chosen to be a slave in the foreign land of Babylon because he was intelligent, bright, handsome and of noble birth.

The Refining Valley of Transformation – Because He Promised

What purpose did the king have in bringing these young men to Babylon? Daniel 1:4-5 _____
_____
_____

There were many young men taken; we are only introduced to four of them: Daniel, Hananiah, Mishael and Azariah (Daniel, Shadrach, Meshach, & Abednego). I cannot help but wonder if the rest of those chosen refused to trust God in the midst of these horrible experiences. Maybe they listened to the voice of the devil and allowed themselves to be alienated from the God who loved them.

The Babylonians had captured the best young men that Israel had, the seed of kingship, in an attempt to destroy their future and to bring them into a place of servitude. Right now, the devil would also love to destroy the best that God has. He looks for those who have the greatest potential, and when they are subjected to the purifying fires of trials, he tries to take them captive to do his will. Whose voice will you listen to?

Daniel, Shadrach, Meshach, and Abednego listened to the voice of God, but they were not asked to do easy things. They trusted God even when faced with inevitable destruction.

Read Daniel chapter 3.

Who came forward and tattled on Shadrach, Meshach, and Abednego? Daniel 3:8 _____

How did the king respond? Daniel 3:13-15 _____
_____
_____

How did the three young men reply? Daniel 3:16-18 _____
_____
_____

If I put myself in their situation, I think I would be wondering where God was in all this mess. I would be thinking about everything I had gone through in the last few years and my faithfulness to God, and I would be wondering if God had abandoned me or if he even cared about what was happening in my life. Thankfully these three men, did not respond like that, instead they gave testimony that even if God did not choose to preserve their lives, they would never abandon their God to worship another. Wow!

We are familiar with the story and know that the king in his anger heated the furnace seven times hotter than usual and ordered the three men to be thrown inside to die. They were cast inside, but they were seen walking around. The only things affected by the intense heat were the ropes that had bound them. Not only were they walking around inside the fiery furnace, but everyone could see a fourth man with them, and he had the appearance of a Son of God!

God's presence was with them in their trial, protecting them and comforting them. It was not God's will for them to be destroyed at the hand of King Nebuchadnezzar and unless God allows something to happen, it will not happen. Remember, we have a sovereign, all-powerful God.

As a result of the faith of these men, King Nebuchadnezzar saw the power of God and offered praise to him. What did the king say about the men in Daniel 3:28?_____
_____

The Blessing

They were slaves in a foreign land, but they were exactly where God wanted them to be. They yielded to God's will and served Him faithfully in their captivity.

Daniel was placed by God in a position of leadership in this foreign land and served under three different kings. Daniel was an old man, probably around 80 years old, when he was forced to make a decision about whether to obey the king's edict which prohibited him from praying to God.

Read Daniel chapter 6.

What question did the king ask Daniel the morning he went out to see if Daniel had survived the night with the lions? Daniel 6:20 _____

_____

Ah, Daniel served an all-powerful sovereign God, who could do anything! He could have even prevented Daniel from ever being thrown into the lion's den in the first place. Isn't that what we ask of God most of the time? "Lord please keep us safe from all harm." We want God to keep us from the hard things, but the greater miracle is when God shows up big in the middle of our trial!

According to Daniel 6:23, why had Daniel been spared? _____

From the time that Daniel was a young man and was carried captive into the land of Babylon, he lived as a slave. He never returned to his homeland or to his family. He served at least three reigning kings. He continued to serve God faithfully in the middle of a life that probably didn't make any sense to him.

We might be tempted to ask God why he allowed such difficulty in Daniel's life. It's the same question we often ask in our own trials. Surely God could find an easier way to accomplish His will, but our All-knowing, Sovereign, Father God knows what is needed to accomplish the work in our lives and in the lives of others.

The rest of the book of Daniel is filled with wondrous visions of things to come. God revealed to Daniel the great mysteries of events in the future! Maybe it was this life of exile that allowed Daniel's relationship with God to grow in such a way that God could trust him with these profound and important revelations. The angel, Michael, appeared to Daniel in chapter 10 and told him that he was highly esteemed. Imagine that! Daniel was highly treasured by God, even though on the surface, the circumstances seem to say that Daniel had been abandoned by God.

One of my favorite stories about Daniel shows up in the Christmas story.

Read Matthew 2:1-12.

Who came to see Jesus? _____

Where had they come from? _____

Why had they come with their gifts? _____

What had led them to Jesus? _____

This is the part I love: Babylon is East of Israel, and these were wise men who studied the stars. When you read about Shadrach, Meshach, and Abednego, do you remember who tattled on them to the king?

Throughout the book of Daniel, there are many references to the king seeking advice from magicians, enchanters, sorcerers, and astrologers. In Daniel 2:24, they are called the "wise men" of Babylon. In chapter 2:48, Daniel was promoted and placed in charge of all the wise men.

So, my heart is delighted when I read in Matthew that the wise men from the East came bearing gifts so that they could worship the one who would be King of the Jews. Daniel had stayed pure in his devotion to God, and in that place of exile in a foreign land, he taught others the truths of God's word. With such clarity and passion, that the truth was retained and explained to the following generations, and 600 years later there was fruit that remained!

Know what you believe about God and believe what you know! Be faithful to Him because He is surely faithful to you!

Just between you and me, God: _____
_____
_____
_____

On coming to the house, they saw the child with his mother Mary, and they bowed down and worshiped him. Then they opened their treasures and presented him with gifts of gold and of incense and of myrrh. Matthew 2:11 (NIV)

Week 3

The Valley of Correction – Because He is My Father

When I find myself in the valley of tears, I find that my source of strength is what I know to be true about God, and I believe it. I make my decisions based on those truths, and I do not fall victim to believing the mirages that often appear in desert places which confuse and lead many people to their deaths. I won't chase after empty things. I choose to believe God and the truths about God that have been revealed to me through Scripture.

For the Lord has comforted His people, and will have compassion on His afflicted ones. ¹⁴Zion says, "The Lord has abandoned me; The Lord has forgotten me!" ¹⁵"Can a woman forget her nursing child or lack compassion for the child of her womb? Even if these forget, yet I will not forget you. ¹⁶Look, I have inscribed you on the palms of My hands; your walls are continually before Me. Isaiah 49:13b-16

God loves with a love that is greater than that of a nursing mother for her baby. He says that He will not forget us! We are inscribed on the palms of His hands. In light of what we know about the cross and the cruel pounding of nails into his hands, clearly, his love for us is engraved upon His hands.

It is this same great love that compelled Him to provide the way of our salvation and caused Him to seal us until the day of redemption with the gift of His Holy Spirit, who makes His dwelling within us. We belong to Him, and He loves us sacrificially.

It is also His great love for us that causes Him to promise to transform us, not willing to leave us as we are, but to make us more like Him! And because of this promise to transform us, He is not willing to let us continue in sinful habits or choices. His love for us motivates Him to correct us when we sin.

There may be times when we find ourselves in the valley of tears due to sinful patterns in our lives, and our Father who loves us very much has brought us there to bring us to a place of repentance. While no punishment seems pleasant at the moment, it will yield a harvest of righteousness.

If you are a parent, grandparent or teacher, you understand that discipline happens **because** you care about the child, not because you don't care. It is because you care that you swat a child's hand when they repeatedly reach for something that is hot or poisonous. We take dangerous things far from their reach, even if they cry and throw a temper tantrum about it. We actively train and discipline throughout their childhood. We stay involved in all the details of their lives because we love them; we have a goal that one day they will live wisely in this world. We want them to excel and do well because they have learned to make good choices. We endure the angry, hateful looks and outbursts, knowing that in time our children will have a better understanding as to why they could not have or do whatever it was that we denied them.

Let's read Hebrews chapter 12:1-13

I absolutely love that this rich passage in Scripture begins with a reminder to keep our eyes on Jesus. He is the author and the finisher of our faith. We are told to keep our focus on Him. Again, we need to know what we believe about Jesus and believe what we know. When we are weary and feel like giving up, it is

His example that will breathe courage into our hearts. As the only begotten Son of God, Jesus left us the example of obedience!

The next few verses draw our attention to discipline that will come from the hand of our loving Father. Never forget or separate the fact that it is because He loves us that He corrects us. He wants us to live in holiness and experience His full blessing and work in our lives. When we choose to sin, to make unholy choices, He will discipline us. Verse 10 says that God will discipline us for our benefit, so that we may share in his holiness.

We are well aware of just how much our children enjoy being disciplined—NOT! It's not something that anyone enjoys. In the process of being disciplined, we are confronted with our wrong action or attitude. We are forced to face up to our wrong choice, and we are usually embarrassed by it; sometimes we even have to face the fact that our decision hurt other people. Once we have owned up to the wrong thing that we did, we often need to apologize and ask for forgiveness. This act is one that produces humility in our hearts and develops compassion for others when they fail.

If we respond to the voice of the one correcting us and we acknowledge the wrong, confess it and ask forgiveness, then the process of discipline is complete.

"Wait just a minute!" you might say, "It wasn't that easy for me!"

If God's discipline in your life was a lot harder than what I just described, consider two things. First, if you do not listen to the voice of the one convicting you of your sin and you continue to forge ahead creating your own way and living in unholiness, then the discipline of the Lord will become stronger and more painful to keep you from walking further down the path of destruction. So, yes, sometimes the hand of the Lord is quite painful, but as we will see from Scripture in our lessons this week, God is patient, and He warns and brings conviction long before he applies His strong arm.

Secondly, note that there are often consequences to our sinful choices. We are free to make choices, but we cannot choose the consequences. Consequences are not magically erased because we have confessed our wrong and have asked God to forgive us. If you have stolen something, you may still go to jail or be forced to make restitution. If you contracted a disease in an immoral relationship, your body would still bear the consequences of that disease. Sometimes, we want to be angry at God for the results of our actions. Scripture gives us ample verses which teach the spiritual principle; you reap what you sow.

Indeed, they sow the wind and reap the whirlwind. Hosea 8:7a

The one who sows injustice will reap disaster… Proverbs 22:8a

Don't be deceived: God is not mocked. For whatever a man sows he will also reap, ⁸because the one who sows to his flesh will reap corruption from the flesh, but the one who sows to the Spirit will reap eternal life from the Spirit. Galatians 6:7-8

Yes, indeed God forgives; it is His nature to forgive and restore, but He doesn't often interrupt the natural laws and the consequences of sin. The impact of the consequences of sin can last a lifetime—consequences should not be confused with God's discipline. God in His kindness will give us His grace to endure and live through the trials that come as a result of natural consequences. He will still complete

His work in us, and He will use those consequences to accomplish His will in our lives or in the lives of others.

Why is our world so full of suffering and destruction? God's design for our world has been broken by sin. He designed man to be his image bearer, to reflect the glory of God! Sin brought death into the world. As sin increases, depravity increases and the consequences of sin abound. Do not blame God for the suffering in the world, blame sin. God has made a way to restore the broken: he sent His Son to make the way for redemption. God's power, His love, His presence and His peace make it possible for us to live in this broken world. God's discipline in our lives keeps us from experiencing more suffering from sin!

We need to be thankful for his discipline. He gives it because He loves us. It doesn't seem pleasant at the moment, but in due season, we will reap a harvest of righteousness!

No discipline seems enjoyable at the time, but painful. Later on, however, it yields the fruit of peace and righteousness to those who have been trained by it. Hebrews 12:11

So we must not get tired of doing good, for we will reap at the proper time if we don't give up. Galatians 6:9

I really like the way the passage in Hebrews 12 describes the discipline of the Lord, and its conclusion.

Therefore strengthen your tired hands and weakened knees, ¹³and make straight paths for your feet, so that what is lame may not be dislocated but, healed instead. Hebrews 12:12-13

We are to strengthen our tired hands, which reminds me of Nehemiah's prayer in Nehemiah 6:9, **"They were all trying to frighten us, thinking, 'Their hands will get too weak for the work, and it will not be completed.' But I prayed, 'Now strengthen my hands.'"** (NIV)

We need God to strengthen our hands for the work that He has for us to do and we need to strengthen our weakened knees. Psalm 95:6 says, **"Come, let us worship and bow down; let us kneel before the LORD our Maker. For He is our God, and we are the people of His pasture, the sheep under His care."**

For this reason, I bow my knees before the Father ¹⁵from whom every family in heaven and on earth is named. ¹⁶I pray that He may grant you, according to the riches of His glory, to be strengthened with power through His Spirit in the inner man, ¹⁷and that the Messiah may dwell in your hearts through faith. I pray that you, being rooted and firmly established in love, ¹⁸may be able to comprehend with all the saints what is the length and width, height and depth of God's love, ¹⁹and to know the Messiah's love that surpasses knowledge, so you may be filled with all the fullness of God. Ephesians 3:14-19

Strong hands, strong knees, and a straight path.

I am teaching you the way of wisdom; I am guiding you on straight paths. Proverbs 4:11

God—He clothes me with strength and makes my way perfect. ³³He makes my feet like the feet of a deer and sets me securely on the heights. ³⁴He trains my hands for war; my arms can bend a bow of

bronze. **³⁵You have given me the shield of Your salvation; Your right hand upholds me, and Your humility exalts me. ³⁶You widen a place beneath me for my steps, and my ankles do not give way. Psalm 18:32-36**

And whenever you turn to the right or to the left, your ears will hear this command behind you: "This is the way. Walk in it." Isaiah 30:21

Strong hands, strong knees and a straight path, so that which is lame may not be dislocated, but healed instead.

We are lame, ladies; we walk with a limp—a weakness toward sin—but when we walk with strong hands, strong knees and on the straight path, our limp is healed!

God can reach down and dislocate the joint, causing us great pain if we choose to ignore His guidance and commands. You can picture the Great Shepherd who would choose to break the leg of a wandering lamb to teach it to stay close and to protect it from the unseen dangers. If a lamb wouldn't stay with the shepherd, but wandered away into danger, he would have his leg broken and then experience the tender care of the shepherd as it healed. Once the disciplined lamb healed, it would be cured of his habit of wandering into danger, and he would stay close to the shepherd.

Hebrews 11:33-34 is right in the middle of the chapter we often call the "Hall of Faith." It is like God's brag book describing ordinary men and woman who believed with great faith in the face of impossible situations and their faith pleased God. Hebrews 11:33-34 describes some of the miraculous things that God accomplished through the faith of these men and women. **"…who by faith conquered kingdoms, administered justice, obtained promises, shut the mouths of lions, ³⁴quenched the raging of fire, escaped the edge of the sword; GAINED STRENGTH AFTER BEING WEAK, became mighty in battle, and put foreign armies to flight.** (emphasis added)

I have experienced the discipline of the Lord in my life. Thankfully, through the years, I have generally responded quickly to the conviction that He has laid upon my heart. The times that I have resisted his first gentle conviction, I have felt a firmer hand upon my heart. I have heard someone describe the Holy Spirit as the "hound dog of heaven." I like that description because it is accurate. You can run away from his conviction, but He will follow you. Psalm 139 says that there is nowhere we can hide from His presence!

One time, I felt the conviction of God to make something right with a friend, and I argued with the Lord over a period of three months. I tried to escape the conviction, but I heard from God in every sermon, and He kept saying the same thing! One Sunday morning, my Sunday School teacher taught Hebrews, chapter 12, about the discipline of the Lord on those He loves. At that moment, I felt like God made it very clear that I either obey or experience His discipline. I obeyed! I love that the Spirit of God dogs us with a heart of love.

As a loving Father, God stays involved in our lives. He keeps his attentive eye upon us because He has a desire that others will see Him in us. He wants to transform us and use us to accomplish great things for Him. He doesn't want us to miss out on all that He has planned for us, and He certainly doesn't want us to experience the suffering that accompanies disobedience. His correction keeps us from further suffering!

We all, with unveiled faces, are reflecting the glory of the Lord and are being transformed into the same image from glory to glory; this is from the Lord who is the Spirit. II Corinthians 3:18

Thank you, Father, that you are transforming us into your image. Thank you that when we choose unholiness, you discipline us as our loving Father. You have not left us to our own sinful natures to grow into bratty, self-centered members of your family. We belong to you, and we represent you in this world. And you are working to transform us!

LORD, happy is the man. You discipline and teach from Your law. Psalm 94:12

Do not despise the LORD's instruction, my son, and do not loathe His discipline; for the LORD disciplines the one He loves, just as a father, the son he delights in. Proverbs 3:11-12

In Revelation 3, the Bible describes the church of God as thinking it is okay without the need for any correction. Did you know that the name Laodicea means "the right of the people" or "people's rights"? Doesn't that sound like a good description of people in our time? To this church, the bride of Christ, Jesus said, "You think you have it all, that you don't need anything, but in reality, you are wretched, pitiful, poor, blind and naked." That is God's description of His church in the last age, hardened hearts toward the voice of God in their lives. They are in a desperate place, far from pleasing God, and content to stay there. In Revelation 3:19, Jesus says, **"As many as I love, I rebuke and discipline. So be committed and repent."** I want to embrace his discipline as an act of love on my behalf. I want to have ears to hear what the spirit says in my life! I want to respond to his conviction!

Ladies, let's pray and ask God to send His Spirit to be a hound dog in our lives, convicting and correcting us when we are wrong. Let's be thankful for the Lord's discipline in our lives and pray that our hearts would be tender enough to respond with repentance and obedience. We don't want to stand before Christ, naked, pitiful, poor and blind. We want to stand before him clothed in His robes of righteousness with a heart purely devoted to Him.

Day 1

He Speaks to Me, Am I Listening?

"The LORD spoke these commands in a loud voice to your entire assembly from the fire, cloud, and thick darkness on the mountain…" Deuteronomy 5:22a

I have heard people say that understanding the Old Testament is difficult. But it is really just one long, beautiful love story. It is God pursuing the sinful heart of man.

The book of Genesis begins with the creation of Adam and Eve. Created in the image of God, they experienced His presence among them and His life within them. But then sin entered the world and death through sin. Sin entered the picture and man experienced the absence of the life of God within him. In Genesis 3, God announced to man the consequences of his sin, but He also made a promise that He would one day send a deliverer who would rescue man from his sin. That verse sets the stage for the rest of the Bible. God began to work in the lives of people, choosing faithful men to create a nation that would be set apart from the rest of the world and their worship of false gods. God was working to establish a nation of people that would worship Him alone, a people who would be faithful to him and would raise their children to know Him so that in the generations to come, He could send the long-awaited promised One who would rescue the hearts of men.

In Genesis, chapter 12, we learn that God would build his nation through the seed of Abraham. In Genesis 35:9-12, God promised Abraham's descendant Jacob that the nation would be born out of his offspring. At that time, God changed Jacob's name to Israel. Israel had twelve sons, and those sons would be known as the twelve tribes of Israel; it would be the descendants of these sons who would be known as the Israelites. It was through this nation of people that the promised One, the Messiah, would come.

Most of the Old Testament is the history of this nation of people and the messages that God sent to this nation through His prophets or messengers.

One of the most amazing things about this nation of people, which had been set apart by God to be His followers, was that they had heard His voice. Their God, unlike all the false gods of the surrounding nations, was alive and had shown Himself to them by speaking the Ten Commandments to them.

One of the key verses in the Old Testament is Deuteronomy 6:4, **"Listen, Israel: The LORD our God, the LORD is One."** It was a crucial verse to the Israelites because their God spoke to them and they could listen to Him. They were commanded in the Ten Commandments not to make any images of God to worship. They were not to be given over to worshipping an image of something; they were to worship Him by obeying His commands, the things that they **heard** from Him.

After God spoke the Ten Commandments, the people were terrified and begged Moses to speak God's words to them. Throughout the rest of the Old Testament, God would speak to His nation of people through the voices of prophets, men who were given a message by God to deliver to the nation of Israel.

Sometimes, we get bogged down reading the messages from these prophets, but the overarching theme of all these message books is, "Repent; turn back to me!" The nation of Israel would cycle through periods of obedience and then through times of disobedience. They would worship God and God alone, and then they would embrace the false gods of the nations around them. God would warn his people time and time again that if they did not repent and turn back to worship Him, He would send a hostile nation to pillage the land. Remember, God disciplines those whom He loves. For the best interest of the nation and the plan of the coming Messiah, God would discipline the nation when it continued in disobedience. But God always pre-empted his discipline with warnings, because as a loving Father, he gave them opportunities to repent and avoid the discipline.

Jeremiah was a prophet sent by God to warn the Israelites that unless they repented, they would be disciplined.

Read Jeremiah chapter 7.

In verse 13, does God indicate that He had warned this nation in the past? _____

Summarize verses 23-26. _____
_____
_____

God spoke to His people in the days of the Old Testament, they routinely ignored what He told them, and they often endured the hard discipline of the Lord to bring them back to a place of repentance.

After God spoke to Israel through the prophet Malachi and before He spoke again in the New Testament, there is a 400 year time period in which God does not speak to His people. What did God say that He would send in Amos 8:11? _____

John 1:1 is one of my all-time favorite verses, **"In the beginning was the Word, and the Word was with God, and the Word was God."**

I am so thankful that God did not remain silent, but that He brought His Word to us himself, clothed in the flesh of man. Immanuel, God is with us! Mary named her son Jesus, for He had come to save His people from their sin.

The One who comes from above is above all. The one who is from the earth is earthly and speaks in earthly terms. The One who comes from heaven is above all. ³²He testifies to what He has seen and heard, yet no one accepts His testimony. ³³The one who has accepted His testimony has affirmed that God is true. ³⁴For God sent Him, and He speaks God's words, since He gives the Spirit without measure. ³⁵The Father loves the Son and has given all things into His hands. ³⁶The one who believes in the Son has eternal life, but the one who refuses to believe in the Son will not see life; instead, the wrath of God remains on him. John 3:31-36

We have the words of God today in the sacred Scriptures.

II Timothy 3:16-17 All Scripture is inspired by God and is profitable for teaching, for _____ , for _____ , for training in righteousness, ¹⁷so that the man of God may be complete, equipped for every good work.

The beautiful truth here is that our God still speaks to us! The creator God of the universe speaks to us. He speaks to us through His written word, and He uses teachers of the Word to explain and make His words clear to us. He has also placed within us His Holy Spirit to remind our hearts of the truths that He has told us. He speaks to us!

Yes, when we choose to please ourselves and go our own way, disregarding God and His ways, He will speak to us through His Word, correcting and convicting us. If we do not heed His words, He will bring discipline into our lives. Is discipline pleasant? No, it is painful. But, know that if you are experiencing His discipline, you heard His convicting voice and chose to ignore it. Even in this place of discipline, He is waiting for you to repent and turn back to Him. His discipline comes because He loves us; it is not for our destruction! God's purpose in discipline is to turn our hearts away from the sinful path that leads to destruction. He wants to restore us to the path of life!

When Jesus addressed the seven churches in the book of Revelation, he ended each letter with this same statement: **"Anyone who has an ear should listen to what the Spirit says to the churches."**

Let's rejoice that God still speaks to us, and let's pray that our ears stay tuned to the voice of the Holy One, that when we hear Him speak, we will obey!

Just between you and me, God: _____

_____
_____
_____
_____
_____
_____

Day 2

Generational Thinking

Naomi took the child, placed him on her lap, and took care of him. ¹⁷The neighbor women said, "A son has been born to Naomi," and they named him Obed. He was the father of Jesse, the father of David. Ruth 4:16-17

I love today's lesson! It is a reminder to think about the generations that will follow you. I recently watched the movie "Monumental." In that movie, it is pointed out that when the Puritans separated from the Church of England and made plans to escape, they had a 500-year plan to build a new democracy and to evangelize the world. What struck me in that statement was that this group of people had been, and were enduring, great persecution, yet their goal was not to just escape the immediate suffering, but rather to live purposefully for the next generation. They were living in such a way as to benefit the next generation! What an amazing thought.

It was challenging to settle in a new country; their struggles, their pain, their sacrifices, their losses… they were all real, and they were painful and hard, but the Puritans were willing to endure it all because they had a goal that their life would provide a foundation for the next generation to do more for God.

The Blessing

I find this type of thinking absent today in our American culture. Maybe in financial arenas, we find some forward thinking, trying to leave fortunes for future generations, but I rarely hear of personal sacrifices to leave a spiritual legacy to our children. Sacrifices being made in our lives for the purpose of our children seeing the glory of God in our lives and to be drawn to Him.

Today, I want us to consider the life of Elimelech and Naomi. It will be just a brief examination of their lives, but hopefully, it will be a lesson in generational thinking and God's redemption.

During the time of the judges, there was a famine in the land. A man left Bethlehem in Judah with his wife and two sons to live in the land of Moab for a while. ²The man's name was Elimelech, and his wife's name was Naomi. The names of his two sons were Mahlon and Chilion. They were Ephrathites from Bethlehem in Judah. They entered the land of Moab and settled there. Ruth 1:1-2

This event happened during the time of the _____ .

One of the summary statements about this period of the judges is found in Judges 21:25, **"In those days there was no king in Israel; everyone did whatever he wanted."** I find that statement interesting; there wasn't a king, but God was ruling the nation through Judges, and He was speaking to the nation through His prophet, Samuel. The nation had knowledge of God's laws, but they chose to live as they pleased. Because of this, this time period in Israel's history is a cycle of **obeying God - receiving His blessings; ignoring God - being disciplined**; **repenting**; and then **obeying God again**.

Moses had given the Israelites the Words of God, and he told them in Deuteronomy 30 that if they would choose to obey God, then God would bless them in their new land. If they didn't, they would experience great hardships. In Deuteronomy 30:19-20, God says, **"I call heaven and earth as witnesses against you today that I have set before you life and death, blessing and curse. Choose life so that you and your descendants may live, ²⁰love the LORD your God, obey Him, and remain faithful to Him. For He is your life, and He will prolong your life in the land the LORD swore to give to your fathers Abraham, Isaac, and Jacob."**

In Ruth chapter one, we learn that there is a famine in the land. That is our first clue that the nation of Israel is not following God at this time. God's blessing isn't upon the land; the nation is being disciplined. The correct and proper response to discipline is repentance, a humbling of our hearts before God.

Elimelech's response was to do what? _____

At first glance it may seem like Elimelech is protecting his family by taking them away from the famine. But Elimelech has chosen not to repent and seek God in the midst of the famine, instead he chose to 'solve the problem' his own way, by taking his wife and children to a foreign country.

Where does he go? _____

He chose to go to the foreign land of Moab, where people worshipped false gods and idols.

How long did he plan to stay there with them? Ruth 1:1 _____

How long did they stay? Ruth 1:4 _____

Elimelech had a choice to make, he could obey God and repent, and by doing so, choose life for himself and his descendants, or he could choose to do what seemed right in his eyes, which in the end would lead to death. Elimelech made his choice to walk by sight and not by faith. He refused to believe and trust God, and in doing so, he made a choice that would destroy his life and the lives of his sons.

Naomi's husband Elimelech died, and she was left with her two sons. Ruth 1:3

Generational thinking causes us to make decisions that are not based on their immediate effect on us, but on the long-term impact the decision will have on our children and their children. Elimelech's decisions also influenced his widow's decision-making process. Naomi didn't return to Israel immediately after her husband's death. This was not just a dad who disobeyed and compromised; this was a family of compromise.

Her sons took Moabite women as their wives: one was named Orpah and the second was named Ruth. After they lived in Moab about 10 years, ⁵both Mahlon and Chilion also died, and Naomi was left without her two children and without her husband. Ruth 1:4-5

Oh, the gaping hole in her heart! I am sure that Naomi was absolutely crushed. It was a pain that she had never experienced before in her life. The children, whom Elimelech removed from Israel because of a famine that he feared might kill them, died in a land far from God, both spiritually and physically. Lives lived in compromise. Far from God. You have heard it said and it is true, "Sin will always cost you more than you intended to pay, will take you further than you intended to go, and will keep you longer than you intended to stay."

When we choose to make decisions based on what seems right in our own eyes, we will make choices that lead to destruction in our lives. God's word has the blueprint by which we need to live. We need to believe His word and obey His word, not because He is a tyrant God who is trying to make our lives miserable if we try to have fun, but because as our creator God, He loves us and wants us to experience the fullness of life. That can only be accomplished when we allow the life of Christ to live through us. His Words and His commandments are for our good, for our benefit, and when we choose to follow them, we are choosing life! It doesn't mean that we won't experience hard things in our lives. We know that from what we have already studied, but when we choose to live according to what is right in our own eyes, we are inviting God's hand of discipline upon our lives and also our children's lives. Why would we want to **ask** for discipline? This is one kind of trouble that we can choose to avoid!

Elimelech made wrong choices, and it cost him his life and the lives of his sons. In God's kind hand of redemption, he saw a broken woman's heart and her recognition that God had brought this desert experience in her life, and that He was drawing her back to Himself and to the land of Israel. He blessed her with the loyalty of Ruth, her daughter-in-law who left her homeland to unite herself to Naomi. He showed Himself faithful to Naomi with the provision of Boaz as Ruth's kinsman redeemer. Boaz and Ruth married and gave birth to a son whom they named Obed. Obed would father a son named Jesse and Jesse would have a son named David, KING David, I should add. And generations later, from the line of David, Jesus, the Savior, would be born.

God's plan is always so much better than ours! We need to pray for the courage to obey His word as we hear it! When we choose life, we are choosing life for ourselves and for our children! Let's start to live beyond ourselves and our own comfort, and live for the lives of those who come behind us!

The Blessing

Just between you and me, God: _____

_____
_____
_____
_____
_____

Day 3

Against Thee and Thee Only

Against You—You alone—I have sinned and done this evil in Your sight. So You are right when You pass sentence; You are blameless when You judge. Psalm 51:4

David, the man that God describes as being someone after his own heart, had sinned a great sin. He had committed adultery with Bathsheba, conceived a child, and had Uriah, Bathsheba's husband, murdered on the battlefield to cover up his sin. Wow! How could this ever be a man be after God's own heart?

Let's look at the account of Nathan confronting King David. Read II Samuel 12:1-15.

What was David's reaction to the parable that Nathan told him about the man who took the lamb that belonged to the poor man? _____
_____

What punishment did David say should be delivered to the man who committed such a great atrocity?
_____
_____

When Nathan told David that He was the man in the parable and repeated all of David's "private" sin back to him along with God's condemnation for these sins, how did David respond? _____
_____
_____

David didn't deny the truth. He didn't try to weasel out of the situation, he didn't shift the blame to Bathsheba; he accepted the full responsibility for his actions. King Saul, who had been the king before David, had a lot of excuses when the prophet Samuel had confronted him in his sin, and it was for that reason that God saw fit to remove His blessing from Saul's kingship. When King David was confronted with his sin, he knew that God had sent Nathan and He owned up to his own sin. By admitting his wrongdoing, he was accepting the death sentence that he had already pronounced upon the offender in the parable. David knew that his offenses were worthy of death.

What was God's response to David's confession? II Samuel 12:13b _____

God's mercy and grace were extended to David and God did not require his death. He would, however, take the life of the baby. David's heart was broken with this news and begged God for the life of the child.

We may question why the baby died when it was David who had sinned, but we need to understand that our decision to ignore the commands that God has given us will bring pain and suffering to others. We have all experienced this harsh reality—that the consequences of other people's sins hurt us and others. David's sinful choices had brought pain and suffering to Bathsheba, caused Uriah's death, and it also brought the death of his newborn son. Do not believe the devil's lie that your decision to sin only affects you.

Every morning that David woke up, he was reminded that God's mercies were new every morning. He had experienced God's mercy in forgiveness and God's grace in life!

Let's read Psalm 51. This is the psalm that David wrote after being confronted by Nathan the prophet.

Does David accept personal responsibility for his sin? _____

In verse 7, David asks God to purify him and wash him as white as snow, then in verse 8, David asks God to let him hear joy and gladness. David's heart had been guilt-ridden and miserable while he tried to keep his sin hidden from others, and strangely he believed it was hidden from God.

How does Psalm 32:3-4 describe the condition of David's heart when he harbors unconfessed sin?
_____

Bless the Lord for also giving us the whole Psalm. How does David describe his heart after he has confessed his sin to God? _____

While confrontation of our sin is never pleasant, it is God's precious gift to us. He wants us to confess and ask for forgiveness so that he can restore His peace to our hearts. God's mercy is one of the most amazing things ever! It is hard to explain to others, but when we know that our hearts are right with God, His unexplainable peace fills our hearts!

On occasion, some people say, "I know that God has forgiven me, but I cannot forgive myself." Was your sin more offensive to you than it was to God? Your sin offended a holy God and if He could forgive you than your refusal to forgive yourself indicates a heart of pride. Our hearts are desperately wicked, but when our hearts condemn us 1 John 3:20 reminds us that God is greater than our hearts!

After removing him, He raised up David as their king, of whom He testified: "I have found David the son of Jesse, a man after My heart, who will carry out all My will." Acts 13:22

When I read that verse about David, I picture David pursuing God. The word "after" can mean "similar in likeness" but it can also mean "pursuit," or a "goal." I like to picture that God chose David, not because He was perfect, but because he would pursue God's heart. He would obey. Yes, he sinned, but he was confronted, he confessed, and David was restored and continued to seek God. Don't give up. Wherever you are in your life, God is a God who pursues us to forgive us! That is His nature. That is why He sent Jesus, to provide a way to forgive us. The devil would like to convince us that if we have fallen, we cannot get up, but that is a lie! God forgives and restores. Keep going **after** God's heart!

Just between you and me, God: _____
_____
_____

Day 4

Muttering Against God

". . . Why then do you exalt yourselves above the LORD's assembly?" Numbers 16:3b

This week in our study we are looking at examples in Scripture of great trials that have come into people's lives as a result of their sin, and the disciplining hand of God upon them. These tests come into our lives because of sinful choices that we have made and because of our refusal to yield our will to the will of God. His deep love compels Him to discipline us so that He can restore us to fellowship and continue the work that He has planned in and through us.

Today, I want us to spend a few minutes looking at Korah. We learn in Exodus 6:16-25 that Korah was a first cousin to Moses and Aaron. They were all from the tribe of Levi, and the Levites were given specific responsibilities regarding the tabernacle.

What responsibilities did the Levites have according to Numbers 1:50-51 and Numbers 3:5-13? _____
_____
_____

This was a tribe set apart to do the work of the Lord. They set up the tabernacle, took it down when it was ready to move, and they were appointed to help Aaron and his sons carry out their priestly responsibilities. They had a job to do, a calling from the Lord.

Read Numbers 16.

According to Numbers 16:1, who was the man spearheading this rebellion? _____

Korah and his descendants had been given a unique job to serve the Lord at the tabernacle. According to Numbers 16:8-10, what else did Korah think he deserved? _____
_____

Korah was greedy for more power, more responsibility, and more honor. He wanted something that God had given someone else. This is what envy is: desiring someone else's blessings. Korah wasn't content with what God had given him, he wanted more. Once Korah had the idea that he deserved more, he influenced many people around him by talking about it and eventually was able to rally a group of 250 people who agreed with him. Just because you can find other people who agree with you on something doesn't necessarily make it right.

Korah brought his discontentment to Moses and challenged his authority. He questioned whether or not God had chosen only one person, Moses, to be a spokesperson. God was not pleased with Korah! When Korah and his followers dared to actually bring their offerings and stand at the door of the tent of meeting, God showed up with fury and power!

God destroyed Korah and his followers by opening up the earth and swallowing them alive. Korah was a Levite and had been given a specific role to perform before the Lord, but he wasn't satisfied with that, he wanted more. He didn't think that God's choice of a leader in Moses or Aaron was necessarily the best choice. He was guilty of presumption and pride. He was severely disciplined for his sins.

I find this example of God's discipline near to my heart as I have found myself active in churches, schools, and ministries where I haven't always agreed with the leadership. I have been vocal at times with my disappointment or disagreement with them and I find this account convicting. God places those whom He desires in places of leadership. He places me where He would have me function. I don't want to get caught up in the sins that destroyed Korah and his followers.

Read Psalm 84. This is a Psalm written with the sons of Korah in mind. This is actually the Psalm that contains the key verses of our study, verses 5-7: **"Happy are the people whose strength is in You, whose hearts are set on pilgrimage. ⁶As they pass through the Valley of Baca, they make it a source of springwater; even the autumn rain will cover it with blessings. ⁷They go from strength to strength; each appears before God in Zion."**

Instead of being greedy for the leadership roles, what is the attitude that Psalmist says should be in our hearts when we serve God? Psalm 84:1-2, 10 _____
_____

Korah and his children learned the hard way to trust God and to be content with God's leading in his life. The generations that came after him could learn from his example, and be thankful and satisfied to just be a *doorkeeper* in the house of the Lord. It was better to have a small job in the presence of God than to dwell in luxury with the wicked.

There are no "big" or "small" jobs with God; there are only faithful or unfaithful people doing what God has called them to do. We want to be faithful people completing the works that God has ordained for us to do. We want to avoid trials in our lives that come because of a heart hardened toward obeying God!

Just between you and me, God: _____
_____
_____
_____
_____

Day 5

Common or Holy?

**You must distinguish between the holy and the common, and the clean and the unclean…
Leviticus 10:10**

In our study today, I want to look at Samson, a man who had been chosen by God at birth to be a deliverer for Israel.

Read Judges 13.

The Blessing

Was Samson's conception a miraculous gift from God? _____

Before Samson was even born, did his mother have to abide by standards of separation? _____

Was he to be raised as an ordinary boy or as a boy set apart as holy to God? _____

Do you suppose that Samson's home life would be different than that of other boys in his neighborhood? _____

What were some of the restrictions mentioned in verses 4-5? _____
_____
_____

Did God reveal the work that He had planned for Samson to accomplish? What did God say in verse 5?
_____
_____
_____

The Angel of the Lord had appeared to a barren woman and promised that she would conceive. The boy to whom she would give birth would be a Nazarite, set apart for God's purposes, from birth.

Numbers 6 gives a more detailed explanation of what would be involved in taking a Nazarite vow. Basically, this vow was a commitment to separate from common life for a period of time, restricting contact with all products of the vine, not cutting the hair and not coming in contact with dead things, all to ask God to work in them or through them to accomplish a specific request. If any of the restrictions were violated, a cleansing process had to be completed, and the vow renewed. In the case of Samson, God chose Samson to be a Nazarite, set apart to be holy unto the Lord, to accomplish the purpose that God had for Samson, to deliver his people from the Philistines.

The word "holy" means to "separate, distinguish, dedicate." The idea is that one thing stands apart from the rest. God is holy; His divine attributes set Him apart from everything else! No one and nothing compares to him.

When we read the story of Samson's life, we will discover that he treated his Nazarite vow casually. He handled it as common, not as holy to the Lord.

Read Judges 14:5-9. What part of the Nazarite vow did Samson's actions violate? _____
_____

According to Judges 6, Samson had an obligation to purify himself and renew his Nazarite vow; Samson knew that he had touched something dead on two occasions, yet kept the knowledge to himself.

Do you think we sometimes keep things to ourselves instead of confessing them to our loving, forgiving God who knows about it already? What usually prevents us from confessing? _____
_____

I can't speak for you, but I know that if I don't want to confess, it is usually because I don't want to change. I still desire the wrong thing and somehow I rationalize that if I don't say anything about it, God will not know or do anything about it. From what you know to be true about God and what we learned when we looked at David's life and his attempt to 'hide' his sin from God, is this type of thinking true? _____

Samson hid the sin from his parents, but he had not hidden the sin from God.

Samson's actions throughout the rest of this Biblical account of his life appear to be motivated by self and selfish pleasure. He seems to have forgotten entirely his vow and the reason that he had been separated as holy to the Lord.

If you are not familiar with the story of Samson, grab a cup of coffee, settle in and read chapters 14-16.

God's purpose was to use Samson to deliver Israel from the Philistines. Was God able to accomplish that mission even though Samson had disobeyed and pursued his own agenda? _____

Did God discipline Samson for violating his Nazarite vow? _____

If so, what did that discipline look like in Samson's life? _____
_____

Did the discipline of God have the desired effect to bring Samson back to a place of recognizing God's purposes? Judges 16:26-30 _____

Write out I Corinthians 6:19-20. _____
_____
_____

Therefore do not let sin reign in your mortal body, so that you obey its desires. ¹³And do not offer any parts of it to sin as weapons for unrighteousness. But as those who are alive from the dead, offer yourselves to God, and all the parts of yourselves to God as weapons for righteousness. Romans 6:12-13

As obedient children, do not be conformed to the desires of your former ignorance ¹⁵but, as the One who called you is holy, you also are to be holy in all your conduct; ¹⁶for it is written, Be _____ , because I am _____ . I Peter 1:14-16

For we are His creation—created in Christ Jesus for good works, which God prepared ahead of time so that we should walk in them. Ephesians 2:10

We have the Spirit of God living within us! We have a Holy calling to accomplish the works that God has ordained for us to do. We are not to offer our bodies to the desires of our flesh and be mastered by them.

So I will make My holy name known among My people Israel and will no longer allow it to be profaned. Then the nations will know that I am the LORD, the Holy One in Israel. Ezekiel 39:7

This verse in Ezekiel tells me that it is possible for something that has been set apart as holy to God (in this verse it is the nation of Israel) to become so common that the name of God is seen as profane, not holy! This never pleases God! In this passage of Ezekiel, God is about to send his discipline upon the nation of Israel.

Ladies, we should not be surprised when God places His hand of discipline upon our lives if we begin to treat our holy calling in life as common. When we treat sin casually and *forget* to repent and ask God to forgive us because we want to continue sinning, we can expect a trial to come. The trial's purpose will be to humble us and bring us to a place of repentance and restored fellowship so that by our holy lives, the entire world will know that He is Yahweh, the LORD, the Holy One!

How long will a discipline trial last in our lives? How long will it take you to humble your heart and return to God? It may take many years to work out the consequences of your sinful choices, but even in the harsh reality of that thought, we have learned from Samson's life that God can still accomplish His work. The picture may not be as pretty as God had planned it to be, but He can still complete His work! He can work all things out to our good according to His purposes.

No discipline seems enjoyable at the time, but painful. Later on, however, it yields the fruit of peace and righteousness to those who have been trained by it. Hebrews 12:11

Just between you and me, God: _____
_____
_____
_____

Week 4

The Valley of His Presence – That I Might Know Him

We are exploring reasons that our Almighty, Holy, Creator, All-powerful, Father God may choose to allow us, His precious children, to endure a season of pain in a valley of tears. If He could prevent it, and He can, how can He be demonstrating love to us by allowing us to suffer? We have already been able to discover two amazing reasons. The first was to purify us, to stir up our lives so that impurities are brought to the surface and can be removed. We discovered that the valley of transformation prepares us for future acts of greatness. God is transforming us! The second reason we explored for why God allows us to suffer is for correction. God is not willing for us to continue down a path of unrighteousness. We are His children, and He will discipline us to bring us back to the place of abundant life which He has promised us. The valley of correction is not pleasant at the moment, but the blessing from God is that it will reap a future harvest of righteousness!

Today we are going to step into the valley of tears to get to know God better. The valley of tears brings me to my knees and supplies the knowledge that I cannot endure this trial on my own. In my own strength I will fail, so I cry out for one to help me, and in this valley place, I discover His presence. I develop an intimate relationship that I didn't even know that I could have. My faith takes root and grows in the valley of His presence.

Think about these two phrases for a moment: The faith of experience, and the experience of faith.

The faith of experience means something entirely different than **the experience of faith**. **The faith of experience** says, because I have experienced it, I believe it. I call this walking by sight.

The phrase **the experience of faith** means that we choose to live by faith and in the process, we are introduced to God in supernatural ways. It is because we have acted in our faith that we have these experiences with God. This is the kind of faith that pleases God.

Now without faith it is impossible to please God, for the one who draws near to Him must believe that He exists and rewards those who seek Him. Hebrews 11:6

It is because we believe in Him that we act and respond in a certain way. Peter stepped out of the boat because He believed that Jesus would sustain him. He believed, and therefore he acted. And when he acted, he experienced the power of God in his life in a way that he had never experienced before.

God has never intended to be just comforting words on a page that we repeat to ourselves when we are alone or frightened. He has designed all along to be in a relationship with us. He desires for us to know Him. He is unsearchable in all his ways, but the challenge He offers us is to pursue Him and seek Him, and in the process, He will reveal Himself to us in a personal, life-changing way.

This takes us back to one of our first weeks of study and the emphasis we made on knowing what we believe and then believing what we know. We want to know Him and He wants to reveal Himself to us. One of the most effective ways for us to know Him better is to increase our faith. When we choose to live according to what we believe, even when it doesn't make sense to our flesh, we will experience God's presence and His strength in ways we did not imagine possible.

The experience of faith.

Peter never got over His experience, his personal encounters with the presence of Jesus.

Peter says in II Peter 1:5, **"...supplement your faith with goodness..."** He is saying to take what you know to be true about God and your faith and add to it goodness. Do the things you know you should do (this whole section of verses is a fabulous description of discipleship!). In verse 9, Peter says that if you aren't doing this, it is because you have forgotten that you had been forgiven. Peter never forgot. He remembered the One who had risen from the dead, the one whom he had seen and touched, and Peter remembered that He had been forgiven for his faithless act of denying Christ. Peter chose to live the rest of his life walking by faith.

When we find ourselves in the midst of a great trial or dark valley, it is hard to imagine that it could ever be anything that we would regard as welcome in our lives. These trials and valleys frighten us. It seems like we beg God to lead us away from such places; we ask that He would always lead us on the smooth, sunny paths of life. We just seem to be more comfortable walking where we can see, without pebbles in our shoes or boulders to climb.

However, if we are never presented with a storm and the opportunity to "step out of the boat," we may never experience the awesome sustaining power of Jesus. If we only walk where it is pleasant, we might never experience the blanket of His peace. There would be so much that we would miss in our pursuit to know God.

I recently heard David Ring, a well-known evangelist, speak and he shared his testimony about having been born with Cerebral Palsy and losing his dad when he was twelve and then losing his mom when he was fourteen. He described an unimaginable valley of pain that lasted for two years after his mom died. She had taken care of him, loved him and had been his security. He said he tried to commit suicide many times during that horrible, dark time in his life. If his mom wasn't alive, he didn't want to be alive. It took a few years before he began to look to God for his strength and purpose, but God remarkably met him where he was. He experienced the presence of God in his life in a real and personal way. He felt called to be a preacher and told his pastor that God was calling him to preach. His pastor told him four times that God would never call him to preach and that God couldn't use someone like him in a pulpit. Recently, David Ring celebrated his 40th anniversary of ministry, having preached in over 7,000 churches across the USA.

I enjoyed hearing his message and his testimony. One of the most shocking things he said was; "I am thankful that God called my momma home because I would not be here today if she were still alive." David had experienced God in such a personal, intimate way during his journey through the valley of tears that his life had been forever changed. He may never have experienced God's sustaining strength in his life had he never experienced such devastating loss.

When I am presented with the opportunity to believe God in the dark places of life, I learn that I no longer need to fear the things that I used to fear. I develop a personal relationship with the One who sustains me. My faith is enlarged, and I walk with confident steps through life because I meet with Jesus, I talk with Him, He is my friend, He is my Savior, and He is all sufficient in my place of need. Just as the roots of the oak tree grow deeper and anchor the mighty tree against the storms, so trials force us to anchor our faith in Jesus, making us stronger for the storms of life.

James, chapter 1, tells us how we should think about trials. Verses 2-4 say, **"Consider it a great joy, my brothers, whenever you experience various trials, ³knowing that the testing of your faith produces endurance. ⁴But endurance must do its complete work, so that you may be mature and complete, lacking nothing."**

Trials can be a source of joy? That is interesting because in Psalm 84:5 we are also told that the man who finds His strength in the God can be happy, even in the valley of tears. Here in the New Testament James is also telling us that trials can be a source of joy because we benefit from them. What benefits did James say would come as a result of trials?

Endurance and maturity.

When we choose to follow God in the midst of a trial, our faith is tried or proven trustworthy. Each time our faith is proven trustworthy, our faith is strengthened. When my faith is strengthened, I take another step of faith. Each time that God supplies the wisdom or strength to persevere through a trial, I know Him better and trust Him more, thus increasing my faith. This develops endurance.

Endurance in the Greek means "cheerful, hopeful, waiting."[1] As we face each trial with faith, enduring the hardship, we allow the necessary passing of time for God to mature us. Maturity doesn't come overnight. A seed planted in the ground bears the blessing of rain and adversity of winds throughout a prescribed time for the plant to reach maturity. Endurance is that hopeful wait; it is the passing of time that is needed for the maturing of God's work.

Endurance is necessary for maturity. James 1:4 says, **"But endurance must do its complete work, so that you may be mature and complete, lacking nothing."** We can welcome a trial with joy, not because it will be a pleasant experience, but because we know that we will be stronger and closer to maturity when it is over.

Now if any of you lacks wisdom, he should ask God, who gives to all generously and without criticizing, and it will be given to him. James 1:5

God doesn't force His wisdom or His ways on us, but He is available and promises to give us wisdom if we ask Him for it. Proverbs 8 is a wonderful description of wisdom. Proverbs 8:35-36 says, **"For the one who finds me (wisdom) finds life and obtains favor from the LORD, ³⁶but the one who sins against me harms himself; all who hate me love death."**

James 1:10-11 describes a man who is rich in himself not acknowledging his need for God's wisdom in the midst of his trial. This man will not endure the trial and mature; instead he will wither and perish. **"...but the one who is rich should boast in his humiliation, because he will pass away like a flower of the field. ¹¹For the sun rises with its scorching heat and dries up the grass; its flower falls off, and its beautiful appearance is destroyed. In the same way, the rich man will wither away while pursuing his activities."**

---

[1] Strong, James, *A Concise Dictionary of the Words in the Greek Testament* (Nashville, TN Abingdon Press, 1890) #5281, page 74

The Blessing

The man who refuses to ask for God's wisdom will be like a plant that withers and its blossom falls off. We all know that when the blossom on a plant matures it develops into the fruit of the plant which contains seeds to produce future plants. So when a man ignores the wisdom of God, seeking instead to face the trials of life on his own, he will not mature and bear fruit.

Blessed is a man who endures trials, because when he passes the test, he will receive the crown of life that He has promised to those who love Him. James 1:12

On the other hand, a man who is able to endure the trial, seeking wisdom from God to endure, will be blessed! He will receive a crown of life! I picture an apple tree "crowned with life" when it is surrounded by little apple trees that have begun to grow from all of the mature fruit that has fallen to the ground around the tree.

When we seek God in our place of trial, He strengthens us and helps us to endure the passing of time, and soon, immaturity is replaced by maturity. Our lives then begin to bear fruit, and that fruit contains seeds which God can use to multiply life many more times! That is something that can make us rejoice!

Trials will come, the testing of our faith. Are we prepared to seek God, asking for His wisdom and strength to endure so that we can mature and bear fruit?

I can't help but think of Jesus and the crown of thorns placed upon His head. Yes, it was a victor's crown, a crown of life! Because Jesus was willing to walk through that valley of suffering, we are all the recipients of life!

Therefore since we also have such a large cloud of witnesses surrounding us, let us lay aside every weight and the sin that so easily ensnares us, and run with endurance the race that lies before us, ²keeping our eyes on Jesus, the source and perfecter of our faith, who for the joy that lay before Him endured a cross and despised the shame, and has sat down at the right hand of God's throne. Hebrews 12:1-2

My faith is matured during trials. My vision and understanding of God grows larger and my understanding a little bit clearer. The joy comes in my heart because I know Him better now. I have discovered Him to be just as He has claimed to be in Scripture.

Even when I go through the darkest valley, I fear no danger, for You are with me; Your rod and Your staff—they comfort me. Psalm 23:4

Day 1

When Did They Know Him?

When they got into the boat, the wind ceased. [33]Then those in the boat worshiped Him and said, "Truly You are the Son of God!" Matthew 14:32-33

"Truly You are the Son of God!" said the disciples. The disciples had just found themselves in a terrible storm, one that had threatened to capsize their boat and take their lives. They had been terrified in that storm. Then Jesus came. This actually frightened them even more than the storm as they thought that He must be a ghost. The disciples were in a dire place; it was desperate, and they were afraid.

Jesus came, and when He did, He spoke to them and told them not to be afraid. Peter's faith was enlarged, his understanding of who Jesus was had increased, and Peter got out of the boat and walked toward Jesus! Imagine the open mouths back in the boat as they gaped in disbelief. The storm was still raging all around them; it didn't actually stop until Jesus got into the boat with Peter and told the storm to stop. At that moment, the disciples were astounded, and they began to worship and say, **"Truly You are the Son of God!"**

If you stop and think about this for a minute, on what occasions did the disciples really get to know Jesus? Sure they knew He was from Nazareth and that He was a teacher who taught with authority, but when were they introduced to Jesus as the second person of the Godhead? The disciples witnessed the power of God at work among them when Jesus did a supernatural work. Have you ever considered that every time Jesus did a supernatural work it was during a crisis?

Read each of these passages and write down what the crisis was and what Jesus did to show Himself as sufficient for the need.

Matthew 8:14-15 _____

_____

Matthew 8:16-17 _____

_____

Matthew 8:23-27 _____

_____

Matthew 9:1-8 _____

_____

List two examples from Matthew 9:18-26 _____

_____

The list could go on and on, but the point being made is that in each instance there was a great trial, there was a moment of need, and it was in those moments that Jesus was able to reveal His supernatural power. He could demonstrate the power of God on behalf of the people in need. The people in need received a glimpse of our all-powerful, loving, Creator God working on their behalf.

The Blessing

Yes, Jesus lived among the people and he taught the disciples, but their faith and their understanding of who God is was grown during times of great trial.

Are you like me; do you pray for safety as we travel, and that sickness and disease will escape us? Do you pray for a life of ease and comfort? I do, and I pray that for my family as well, yet if I understand Scripture correctly, it is during hard times that we are introduced to a God who demonstrates His power, His peace and His presence on our behalf! It is in those trying times that we get to see God! So why do we beg so hard for the path of least resistance? Don't get me wrong, I am not going to start begging for trials, but I think my daily prayer should be that my faith would be enlarged as I recognize God's hand at work in my life!

John 10:14-15 "I am the good shepherd. I know My own sheep, _____
_____
_____
_____
_____

This is an intimate knowledge of Jesus, in the same manner, that God knows Jesus! That is our goal: to pursue Jesus and know Him that well. That won't happen if we only walk on the mountaintops of life; it is in the valley of weeping that Jesus opens our eyes to who He really is!

Trials are the tools that God uses to make Himself known to us in all His Glory! We can rejoice in knowing that He will open the eyes of our understanding.

We fight against trials and hard times, but those may be the times that we have the closest view of God!

Just between you and me, God: _____
_____
_____
_____
_____

Day 2

He Brought Peace

You will keep in perfect peace the mind that is dependent on You, for it is trusting in You.
Isaiah 26:3

The following is the testimony of Brandi Adams, a young mom who walked through a very dark valley of tears.

"On April 29, 2005, the worst thing that can happen to a parent happened. I was driving on a state highway and was in a car accident; my two oldest daughters, Ariel (7) and Valerie (5), were killed on impact. My youngest daughter, Michelle (2), and I were life-flighted to separate hospitals in Columbus."

"I was in and out of consciousness at the scene and had no idea what had happened. It was several hours later while I was in the ER before I was coherent enough to ask about my children. My parents and husband were there and I was told immediately that Michelle was at Children's Hospital and was okay, but they didn't immediately tell me about Ariel and Valerie. When I asked about them and saw the expressions on the faces of the people around me, I knew. By that time I was very medicated, and all emotions were considerably dampened. But I remember this intense ache in my chest, one that was internal and not explained away by broken bones. All I can remember thinking is, "Oh God, Why?!"

For a few days, my short-term memory was very sketchy. It took some time to remember what had happened and the even now trying to remember the couple of weeks that followed, my brain is very foggy. I was on a lot of pain meds for multiple breaks. I barely remember the funeral and visiting hours. One of the few things I remember clearly was insisting that my daughters be buried together. How could you possibly separate in death two children who were so close in life? Humanly speaking, I didn't want my children to be alone.

Having been raised in a Christian, God-loving home all of my life, I knew what Scripture taught. I knew that God does not ask us to understand His ways and we are not expected to comprehend His plans, but that didn't eliminate the questions of "How?" and "Why?" and the all-encompassing, "I just don't understand!" I can't say that I was steeped in prayer in those times, I was so completely numb, but I knew with all of my heart that I was covered in prayer from around the globe. My family and I know people all over this country and around the world, and I knew their prayers were everywhere.

I also knew such a deep peace that it can't be explained. God does indeed provide the peace that "surpasses all understanding." I didn't and still don't know why my girls are gone; I don't know why God chose to take them home at such innocent and young ages. But I do know this: they are with Him. I know that at their funeral several people made a profession of faith. In my mind, I can see my girls running to Jesus with open arms the way they did with everyone they loved, huge smiles with arms wide open, yelling, "Jesus, Jesus!"

Being at peace and grieving are not contradictory; Jesus grieved the loss of his friends and wept. I understood that my pain was natural, it was and is being human, but there can still be peace. I have no doubt that like in the poem "Footprints," Jesus carried me. He allowed me to grieve while He "carried" me through the darkest hours of my life. Was my faith shaken? I really don't think so. I have been blessed with a family who raised me to know God. I don't know how I could have survived the loss of Ariel and Valerie without knowing that they were with the Lord, that He knows and feels everything I feel, that there is nothing I can endure without His strength and that He understands.

I am still at peace; I still grieve. You don't "get over" the loss of your children, but God will and does walk me through it. Whether He is carrying me at the time or walking with me, He's there.

And the peace of God, which surpasses every thought, will guard your hearts and minds in Christ Jesus. Philippians 4:7

Just between you and me, God: _____
_____
_____
_____

The Blessing

Day 3

Who by Faith...

...who by faith conquered kingdoms, administered justice, obtained promises, shut the mouths of lions, ³⁴quenched the raging of fire, escaped the edge of the sword, gained strength after being weak, became mighty in battle, and put foreign armies to flight. ³⁵Women received their dead raised to life again. Hebrews 11:33-35a

I have often heard Hebrews 11 called "God's Hall of Faith." Surely this chapter is a "hall of fame" for men and women who pleased God with their faith. The names of some of our favorite Bible characters are listed in this chapter. While I love reading about these Biblical heroes, I find this a convicting chapter to read because when I begin to consider the details and the circumstances behind each of these people and their decision to trust God in the midst of very dark valleys, I am humbled by my own lack of faith.

For me, it seems so easy to listen to the voice of the devil as He accuses God of being unfair in my situation, of not loving me or of forgetting about me. I can get so wrapped up in the immediacy of my own trouble that I forget that the work God is doing in my valley experience might even be for the benefit of the next generation. I know for myself just how easy it is to default to "faithless" thinking and that is not what I want! I want my mind renewed and transformed so that my default thinking is to always look for God in the midst of whatever dark valley I am walking. I want to seek Him out, tuning my ear to listen for the voice of the One I know and trust, who says in my ear, "This is the way, walk in it." I want to please God with my faith!

According to Hebrews 11:6, what is needed to please God? _____

_____

What is faith? Hebrews 11:1 _____

_____

I understand faith to be what I know and believe to be true about God. I cannot see God, but the reality of my belief changes my behavior. Does that make sense? What I believe to be true about God, even though I cannot see Him, will affect my conduct. That is genuine faith. If I say that I believe something, but my behavior is not changed by that belief, then the argument could be made that I don't actually believe what I said I believed. Belief influences behavior. My actions prove my beliefs.

This chapter is littered with the names of men and women who believed something about God and that belief caused them to behave in ways that proved their belief. They didn't understand all that God was doing, they didn't know how the situations would end, but the one thing they did know was that God was faithful, and they chose to obey and follow God in situations that most people would have thought impossible.

List the names of the people mentioned in this chapter and when you are writing their names think about the situations in which they found themselves and think about their choices to believe God in those impossible situations. _____

_____
_____
_____

This chapter describes two kinds of people who lived by faith: those who lived to see the reward of their faith and those who did not. Today we are looking at those who saw the reward of their faith.

In Hebrews 11:33-35a, write down the miraculous things that were accomplished through the lives of people who chose to believe God and live by faith. _____
_____
_____
_____

One thing comes to mind when I read those wonderful things: serving God is EXCITING! Imagine choosing to believe God in an impossible situation and watching God work a miracle on your behalf! We love the miracle side of the event, but think about the fact that someone, when faced with lions, chose to believe that God would shut their mouths, and God did on their behalf. The miracle is exciting, but I could pass on the experience of seeing lions face to face! You see, we want to see miracles, but rarely do we want to be in a situation that allows God to perform a miracle. We want to stay in the safe zone and watch the lions through the fence at the zoo.

God may allow us to come face to face with lions so that we have the opportunity to choose to believe Him in the impossible situation, so that He can show Himself to us!!

Ladies, I want to quit running in fear from hard things; I want to start seeing God do amazing things. I started praying for some really big things this year, impossible things, because I realized I usually only ask for things that seem possible. God is able to do the impossible; let's start believing that He is God and let our behavior be changed by our belief!

Now to Him who is able to do above and beyond all that we ask or think—according to the power that works in you— [21]**to Him be glory in the church and in Christ Jesus to all generations, forever and ever. Amen. Ephesians 3:20-21**

Just between you and me, God: _____
_____
_____
_____
_____
_____
_____

The Blessing

Day 4

The World Was Not Worthy of Them!

The world was not worthy of them... Hebrews 11:38a

Yesterday we looked at some miraculous results of living by faith. When men and women chose to live by faith, God showed up on their behalf and miracles were accomplished! These men and women believed God in the face of the impossible and God delivered them. The stories make sense to us, and they conclude well. We love happy endings all tied up with a bow!

Today, however, we will be looking at some other heroes of the faith mentioned in this chapter. They are not listed by their name, and by human standards, their stories don't really end well.

Read Hebrews 11:36-38.

Make a list of the afflictions that these faith heroes experienced. _____
_____
_____
_____
_____

These men and women chose to believe God in the face of the impossible and God did not show up and deliver them from their affliction. We don't understand this. Why would God show up and rescue some people and not others? Does He love some more than others? Did some have more faith?

No, what we know to be true about God is that He is faithful in His love to us, he does not waver in His love, loving us more one day and less on other days. He promises to work all things together in our lives for good. We know that God desires to reveal Himself to us and that our faith in Him pleases Him. We know that He will sustain us in our trial, holding our hands and strengthening us for the task.

So, when we choose to believe God, and we act upon that belief, we demonstrate our faith in God. This pleases Him. If He chooses to act supernaturally and reveal Himself to all those around, we will rejoice and thank Him; but if He chooses not to reveal Himself to the crowds and does not end the trial, may we walk on with confidence, embracing the personal encounter He has chosen for us. That is an act of faith designed for our private growth, not for the world to understand. God describes these dear faith heroes as having more value than the world deserved! They were and are so precious to Him.

God has not forsaken or abandoned you when you do not experience a miracle on your behalf; open your eyes and look for Him to show up in a personal way. This faith experience is for your personal growth, for you to understand and see God in a closer way!

Just between you and me, God: _____
_____
_____
_____
_____

Day 5

Rumors or Vision?

I had heard rumors about You, but now my eyes have seen You. Job 42:5

Job is one of the first people we think about when we think of someone who experienced great trials and suffering. In a later lesson, we are going to examine the reasons why God allowed Job to endure such a great trial, but today I want to look at the personal result of Job's valley of suffering. How did Job's faith grow in that dark valley place? How did his understanding of God increase during that time?

Write the description about Job or about His attitude from the following verses:

Job 1:1 _____

Job 1:5 _____

Job 1:20-22 _____

In these verses, we can observe that Job was devoted to God in worship, and he had an understanding of God's sovereignty.

A large part of the book of Job is made up of the conversations that Job had with his friends as they tried to tell him that it was because of his sin that God was punishing him. Their advice and understanding of God are logical, but what seems reasonable to man is not necessarily true about God.

Job began questioning God, and he asked for an audience with God in chapter 31.

**If only I had someone to hear my case! Here is my signature; let the Almighty answer me. Let my Opponent compose His indictment. ³⁶I would surely carry it on my shoulder and wear it like a crown. ³⁷I would give Him an account of all my steps; I would approach Him like a prince.
Job 31:35-37**

If you are like me, you can sense a bit of arrogance in Job's complaint; as if God owed him an explanation for the trial.

God responds in chapters 38-41 to Job's request for an audience with Him, and they are some of the most beautiful chapters in Scripture. God describes Himself and His power, and he details His care and maintenance of the universe. Repeatedly, God asks Job if he was present when He was doing all these things. Job's understanding of who God is and His awesome, great power is continually expanded during God's response to Job.

Read Job 40:1-5. How does Job respond to God?_____

_____

_____

_____

The Blessing

God continues to reveal his nature and his character to Job in chapter 41, and after Job hears all of that, he gives another response to God beginning in chapter 42:1-6. **"Then Job replied to the Lord: ²I know that You can do anything and no plan of Yours can be thwarted. ³You asked, 'Who is this who conceals My counsel with ignorance?' Surely I spoke about things I did not understand, things too wonderful for me to know. ⁴You said, 'Listen now, and I will speak. When I question you, you will inform Me.' ⁵I had heard rumors about You, but now my eyes have seen You. ⁶Therefore I take back my words and repent in dust and ashes."**

On a personal level, Job's faith was grown during this great trial. What he had heard about God, he now knew to be true because He had encountered God in a compelling and personal way. Job discovered an all-powerful God who can do as He pleases; Job changed his stance from calling God out and demanding an audience to that of a closed mouth yielded to God's will in his life. As Job's knowledge of God grew, his humility grew.

Job would live the rest of his days with a faith that was rooted in what he knew to be true about God. Nothing could dissuade him now! This trial of faith was a gift from God!

Just between you and me,_____
_____
_____
_____
_____

Week 5

The Valley of Glory – That Others Might See Him

We have been considering reasons why our All-powerful, loving, Father God would allow His precious children to experience the pain and suffering that accompanies a journey through the valley of tears. We have discovered the blessing of a God who has promised to transform us, not willing that we should be left conformed to this world. We have also learned that correction in our life is a blessing from the gracious hand of a loving Father. Also, we have been taught to look for the blessing of His presence in a real and personal way. Our faith grows each time we act on what we know to be true about God, and He proves Himself trustworthy! This is a personal experience, and it is one that is meant to help us know God in a real way.

Today we are looking at another blessing that comes as a result of a journey through the valley of tears. It is similar to the one we talked about last week, but instead of Jesus revealing Himself to us on a personal level for our own faith to be grown, this blessing has to do with Jesus revealing Himself through us for all the world to see His glory! We get to be a reflection of Him in this dark and broken world. This concept of being a light in a dark world is a favorite of ours, but one that is actually very difficult to embrace. We love the idea of Jesus being seen in us, but the events that allow Him to be seen in us have us fussing, complaining and running the other way!

There will be times in our lives when Jesus chooses to allow us to experience great trials so that when others observe our actions and attitudes while we are in that place of suffering, they won't see us, they will see Jesus. Think of Shadrach, Meshach, and Abednego. When they were thrown into the fiery furnace, people marveled because they saw Jesus with them. They did not respond like most people would have when threatened with being thrown into a consuming fire; they did not wither and faint and beg to be saved from such a horrific death sentence. They knew what they believed about God and they knew that it was wrong to worship anyone other than God, and that belief caused them to make radical, faith-motivated decisions which led to them being thrown into the fire. But in that fiery furnace, they acted differently than others had who had experienced that same kind of death sentence. Shadrach, Meshach, and Abednego not only lived, but they also walked around in that fire, and others marveled when they saw one who had the form of God in that fire with them! God was seen in that place of suffering, and He strengthened them to live supernaturally!

A couple of years ago in Schroon Lake, New York, a young man, Graham, was injured in a horse accident. He was married with two small children at the time. He suffered a deep brain injury and was not expected to survive. His sweet wife, Randi, kept a blog online for all of their friends to read about Graham's progress. She was so open and vulnerable in her testimony during this very dark path; it was very hard, and she cried many tears, but she trusted the One who had led her down this dark path. After reading her blog one day, I wrote the following to her. "The Glory of the Lord is being seen in your lives as you walk through this trial declaring God to be faithful and sufficient. This testimony is powerful and supernatural; it is what the world craves to know—that God is real and that He is real during the darkest of days. As we watch you live out our own worst fears, we see God's presence and His sustaining help, and that strengthens our own faith and magnifies the Lord. The promise from God is not that it will be easy—but that He will be with you. Thank you for sharing your story of God's

The Blessing

faithfulness—each day we see the light of God's Glory—Keep your eyes on Him, Randi—we keep praying for you."

Randi Stump, the wife who walked through this dark valley, just published a book about their experience called The Dark Stretch. One of the great blessings that came out of her journey was that others clearly saw God in her life. The glory of God was seen, and as an onlooker, my own faith was encouraged.

Peter wrote to Christians who were going through intense times of suffering and persecution. He didn't just give them a comforting pat on the back and tell them that he hoped it would end soon; he spoke words of encouragement to remind them to stay strong in the midst of the suffering because it was accomplishing something of great value! We will only look at a few verses today, but if you have the opportunity this week, it would be great if you could read the entire book; it will be a blessing to you!

**You rejoice in this, though now for a short time you have had to be distressed by various trials ⁷so that the genuineness of your faith—more valuable than gold, which perishes though refined by fire—*MAY RESULT IN PRAISE, GLORY, AND HONOR AT THE REVELATION OF JESUS CHRIST.*
I Peter 1:6-7**   (emphasis added)

Can you wrap your mind around that? Yes, we will struggle in various trials, and those trials will prove the genuineness of our faith, which is even more valuable than gold; and these trials will result in praise, glory, and honor when others see Jesus in us! Sometimes we mistakenly think that the goal of our salvation was getting us to heaven, but I have heard Major Ian Thomas say, and I agree with him, that "the goal of our salvation was to get God back into man!" When we who belong to Him experience trials, and we choose by faith to live out the things that we know to be true about God, then Jesus is seen in us! That is what we were created to do, be a reflection of His glory!

Therefore, get your minds ready for action, being self-disciplined, and set your hope completely on the grace to be brought to you at the revelation of Jesus Christ. ¹⁴As obedient children, do not be conformed to the desires of your former ignorance ¹⁵but, as the One who called you is holy, you also are to be holy in all your conduct; ¹⁶for it is written, Be holy, because I am holy. I Peter 1:13-16

We are to be obedient as children of God, imitating Him, and setting our hope on the grace that will be brought to us when Jesus is seen in us!

For it brings favor if, because of conscience toward God, someone endures grief from suffering unjustly. ²⁰For what credit is there if you endure when you sin and are beaten? But when you do good and suffer, if you endure it, it brings favor with God. ²¹For you were called to this, because Christ also suffered for you, leaving you an example, so that you should follow in His steps. ²²He did not commit sin, and no deceit was found in His mouth; ²³when reviled, He did not revile in return; when suffering, He did not threaten, but committed Himself to the One who judges justly. ²⁴He Himself bore our sins in His body on the tree, so that, having died to sins, we might live for righteousness; by His wounding you have been healed. ²⁵For you were like sheep going astray, but you have now returned to the shepherd and guardian of your souls. I Peter 2:19-25

If we suffer for doing what is right, that brings favor with God. We have the example of Jesus who had committed no sin and responded in faith when He did not revile those who reviled Him. He did not threaten those who threatened Him. He entrusted Himself to God and to God's justice! We were like sheep that went astray, but we have returned to the Shepherd, the Guardian of our souls!

And who will harm you if you are passionate for what is good? [14]But even if you should suffer for righteousness, you are blessed. Do not fear what they fear or be disturbed, [15]but set apart the Messiah as Lord in your hearts, and always be ready to give a defense to anyone who asks you for a reason for the hope that is in you. [16]However, do this with gentleness and respect, keeping your conscience clear, so that when you are accused, those who denounce your Christian life will be put to shame. [17]For it is better to suffer for doing good, if that should be God's will, than for doing evil. [18]For Christ also suffered for sins once for all, the righteous for the unrighteous, that He might bring you to God, after being put to death in the fleshly realm but made alive in the spiritual realm. I Peter 3:13-18

Dear friends, when the fiery ordeal arises among you to test you, don't be surprised by it, as if something unusual were happening to you. [13]Instead, as you share in the sufferings of the Messiah rejoice, so that you may also rejoice with great joy at the revelation of His glory. [14]If you are ridiculed for the name of Christ, you are blessed, because the Spirit of glory and of God rests on you. [15]None of you, however, should suffer as a murderer, a thief, an evildoer, or as a meddler. [16]But if anyone suffers as a Christian, he should not be ashamed, but should glorify God with that name. [17]For the time has come for judgment to begin with God's household; and if it begins with us, what will the outcome be for those who disobey the gospel of God? [18]And if the righteous is saved with difficulty, what will become of the ungodly and the sinner? [19]So those who suffer according to God's will should, in doing good, entrust themselves to a faithful Creator. I Peter 4:12-19

We should never be surprised by a valley experience of suffering. We are on a pilgrimage here on this earth; this is not our home. Our citizenship is in heaven, and while we are living here, we live as citizens of our heavenly home. When we live otherworldly lives among those who are still dead in their trespasses and sins, we can expect that they won't understand and that they may persecute, harass and be the source of much suffering in our lives. But when we suffer for living right, we should rejoice because the Spirit of Glory and God rests upon us! Isn't that awesome? Just like Shadrach, Meshach, and Abednego, others will "see" God in us! Just as Jesus entrusted Himself to God, we are admonished that we too can entrust ourselves to our faithful Creator!

Be sober! Be on the alert! Your adversary the Devil is prowling around like a roaring lion, looking for anyone he can devour. [9]Resist him, firm in the faith, knowing that the same sufferings are being experienced by your brothers in the world. [10]Now the God of all grace, who called you to His eternal glory in Christ Jesus, will personally restore, establish, strengthen, and support you after you have suffered a little. I Peter 5:8-10

Peter ends this letter to the Christians who were suffering by warning them to be on guard against the Devil who would seek to destroy them. Be aware and on guard against Him. How do you resist him? We are told to be firm in our faith! Know what you believe and believe what you know. Allow what you believe to influence your behavior. We should live differently in this world because we are not of this world.

The Blessing

Now the God of all grace, who called you to His eternal glory in Christ Jesus, will personally restore, establish, strengthen, and support you after you have suffered a little. 1 Peter 5:10

Thank you, God, that you will PERSONALLY restore, establish, strengthen and support us! I had a Pastor who used to say, "All suffering is temporary, even if it lasts a lifetime." Eternity will be free of suffering!

Let us be willing to accept that God in us wants to be seen in the world around us. He is seen in us when we choose to live faith-based lives, making our choices based on our new lives as God's children, being holy because God is holy. When we choose to live holy lives in an unholy world, we shine as lights in a dark world. When we choose to live by faith, we experience the revelation of Jesus Christ! He is seen in us! Woo hoo! That is pretty awesome. Take courage and do not run from trials, but expect that they will come and seek to show God to others in the midst of the trial! They will marvel when they see Him!

Therefore we do not give up; even though our outer person is being destroyed, our inner person is being renewed day by day. [17]For our momentary light affliction is producing for us an absolutely incomparable eternal weight of glory. II Corinthians 4:16-17

Day 1

This Mind in You

Let this mind be in you, which was also in Christ Jesus. Philippians 2:5 (KJV)

If we are going to experience suffering for the purpose of God being seen in us, we need to understand what it means for God to be seen in us. What does that look like, practically speaking? If I quote the Bible a lot and am kind to everyone, is that Jesus being seen in me?

Philippians chapter 2 gives us a picture of God being seen in Jesus and the admonition that we are to imitate the example of Jesus.

List the five things we receive from Christ in Philippians 2:1 _____
_____
_____
_____

Paul says that if we have received these benefits from Christ, then according to Philippians 2:2, we can fulfill Paul's joy by living how?_____
_____
_____
_____

If Christ is our example, there will be some things that we must do as He did; that is the point of imitation or being like-minded. According to Philippians 2:3-4, we are told that we think like Him when we are not being jealous of each other and trying to accomplish things for our own superiority, but rather when we consider others as more important than ourselves.

When Jesus came to earth, did He come because it was the best thing for HIM to do or because it was the best thing for US?

Write out Philippians 2:5._____
_____
_____

You see, Jesus came to serve others, not to be served. Mark 10:45 says, **"For even the Son of Man did not come to be served, but to serve, and to give His life—a ransom for many."**

This servant mindset is contrary to that of the mindset of our natural man. Our old nature is obsessed with self and the exaltation of self. Jesus came, willingly relinquishing his right to honor and took on the form of a servant. He left the visible manifestation of His glory in heaven and clothed Himself in the flesh of man so that He could live as God had created man to live: sinless, obedient to God. He was obedient even to death, the death of the cross. In His obedience, Jesus secured for all mankind the opportunity to have their sins forgiven, and to have the Spirit of God reside inside them. God has sealed us until the day of redemption.

The Blessing

Think about some of the things that Jesus gave up when He came clothed in the flesh of humans. He gave up His right to honor; people did not honor Him here. He deserved honor, but when He came, He did not demand it. He gave up His right to be worshipped as the creator God. Yes, He was the Creator God, but clothed in the flesh of man; people did not recognize Him as so, but Jesus completed the work that the Father gave him to do clothed in the camouflage of flesh, yielding his right to be recognized and worshipped.

Read Philippians 2:5-11.

Jesus lived out perfectly this idea of thinking of others as more highly than yourself. He emptied Himself to be obedient to God's will to secure the salvation of mankind. If Jesus had been concerned with His own honor and prestige, thinking more highly of Himself than others, He would not have completed the work that God had given Him to do. Because Jesus was willing to temporarily lay aside the visible attributes of His Godhead, the Father highly exalted Him.

Let this mind be in you. Jesus humbled Himself, being obedient to death for the purpose of God's work in securing the salvation of man to be accomplished. Jesus served others in humility, He endured the mocking, ridicule and the physical pain, and most incredibly, He became sin for us. He came and lived as God among us; He showed us what God is like and He showed us what a holy life looks like. So if we are going to imitate Jesus, we are going to have to be willing to yield our rights to the will of the Father. We need to be willing to be obedient to do the things that God asks us to do, even to the point of death if that is His plan for our lives. We need to be willing to serve others instead of being served. Not just one-time, but all the time, our lives should be others-oriented.

In John 13, Jesus washed his disciple's feet as an example for us. He said that if He, as our Teacher and Lord washed feet, so should we be willing to serve others. A servant is not greater than His Master. If He was willing to get down and to get dirty to serve others, so then we ought to be willing.

Can you joyfully serve Jesus if you get asked to clean bathrooms? Can you be content in the background making meals for people who are sick? Can you continue to serve a person who insulted or hurt you? Can you serve in a place where no one notices what you are doing? Can you serve others or are you only content when you are being served? Can you serve without recognition or do you need the applause of men for your efforts?

This kind of living is not easy; it is dying to self and its need for preeminence, and yielding your life to Jesus whose Spirit lives within you, who desires to serve others through you. When we accepted Jesus as our Savior, the promise that He made to us was that He would give us new life; out with the old, in with the new. We are new creatures in Christ. We are being transformed into His image and that transformation process will require us to let go of our own "need" for honor and allow the Spirit of God to reign in our mortal bodies! He rules! We belong to Him.

If we experience hardship in this life, it may be because Jesus would like to show Himself to the people around you and He is choosing you to be the vessel with which to demonstrate Him to them. As we yield our "rights" and allow God to be seen in us, we bring light to a darkened world!

Just between you and me, God: _____

_____

_____

_____

_____

Day 2

The Mystery of Job

Then the LORD answered Job from the whirlwind. Job 38:1

I feel like this study would not be complete without a look at Job. His life is the epitome of one who has walked this dark journey through the valley of tears. One of the reasons that Job is such an example to us is that Job did not have the written words of God. He did not have the revealed knowledge of God that we do. He lived in a polytheistic society where exclusive worship of one God was not typical.

Job, with the revealed knowledge that He did have of God, chose to believe what he knew to be true about God in the face of the most horrific events. His faith, what he knew to be true about God, was enough to sustain him through this valley. He could not see God in the agony of his pain, but he was confident that God saw Him and knew the way that he was going.

Look at the following verses and write out Job's description of his pain or his suffering.

Job 2:7-8 _____

Jo 2:11-13 _____

Job 6:2 _____

Job 12:4 _____

Job 16:16 _____

Job 17:1 _____

Job 19:9-20 _____

God required a lot of Job in this valley experience. He was asking him to lay down his health, lay down his family, lay down his business and lay down his reputation. This was a lot to ask; he wasn't just asked to lay down <u>one</u> thing, which would have been hard enough, but he was asked to lay it <u>all</u> down and still trust God. Job's faith, his understanding of God, grew in that dark place. He looked for God and could not find Him, but Job was confident that God had not abandoned him; although Job couldn't see God, he was sure that God knew exactly where he was.

The Blessing

When He is at work to the north, I cannot see Him; when He turns south, I cannot find Him. ¹⁰Yet He knows the way I have taken; when He has tested me, I will emerge as pure gold. ¹¹My feet have followed in His tracks; I have kept to His way and not turned aside. Job 23:9-11

Job's faith declared that although He could not see God at work when he looked for Him, he knew that God was working and that God was fully aware of where Job was. Job was confident that when the trial by fire was over, He would be a stronger, purer person because of the trial. Job had been following after God, not turning to the right or to the left—but pursuing God.

Job did question God. In Job 23:2-5, he said that he wanted to state his case before God. He was confused and in great pain, and He wanted some answers from God. Yet in all this, we are told that Job did not sin. So we must understand then that when we face similar valleys that bring us to our knees, it is not a lack of faith to ask God questions. When Job asked, he always acknowledged the supremacy of God. Look at a few verses that reveal Job's reverence toward God.

Then Job stood up, tore his robe and shaved his head. He fell to the ground and worshiped, ²¹saying: Naked I came from my mother's womb, and naked I will leave this life. The LORD gives, and the LORD takes away. Praise the name of the LORD. ²²Throughout all this Job did not sin or blame God for anything. Job 1:20-22

His wife said to him, "Do you still retain your integrity? Curse God and die!" ¹⁰"You speak as a foolish woman speaks," he told her. "Should we accept only good from God and not adversity?" Throughout all this Job did not sin in what he said. Job 2:9-10

So, I believe that we learn from Job that it is okay to question God when we are in that dark place, but those questions should not be framed in accusations against the character of God. We shouldn't raise our fist and rail against God. That would dishonor God. We are permitted to question, to ask the "why" question that seems to boil out of us when we are in that place, but we also can also learn another great lesson from Job. When God chose to answer Job's questions with a display of His glory, might, and power, Job wished he could have taken His questions back; he was humbled at God's reply and with great humility Job worshipped His Creator God.

The LORD answered Job: ²Will the one who contends with the Almighty correct Him? Let him who argues with God give an answer. ³Then Job answered the LORD: ⁴I am so insignificant. How can I answer You? I place my hand over my mouth. ⁵I have spoken once, and I will not reply; twice, but now I can add nothing. Job 40:1-5

Then Job replied to the LORD: ²I know that You can do anything and no plan of Yours can be thwarted. ³You asked, "Who is this who conceals My counsel with ignorance?" Surely I spoke about things I did not understand, things too wonderful for me to know. ⁴You said, "Listen now, and I will speak. When I question you, you will inform Me." ⁵I had heard rumors about You, but now my eyes have seen You. ⁶Therefore I take back my words and repent in dust and ashes. Job 42:1-6

Job's faith was grown during this valley journey as his understanding of God was enlarged. God used this valley of tears to show Himself to Job in a greater way than Job had ever known or experienced before. This suffering had not come because Job was sinning or needed to be corrected, the trial came because Job served God and was righteous. That kind of math is hard for us to compute, but it is God's math. Personally, this was an experience of faith for Job, and his vision of God increased, but corporately God chose Job to be tried in this way so that Job's righteous response would allow a testimony through the ages for all to see that God is faithful and that He is Sovereign. Because Job was willing to trust God through his valley of tears, we all have the privilege of seeing God better too!

God's glory has been revealed through all the ages through the printed example of Job which God included in the Bible. Job suffered excruciating pain, trusted God in the midst of the darkness and God chose to honor his faith by revealing more of Himself to Job! We are the beneficiaries of this amazing revelation of God with some of the most beautiful, descriptive passages about God in all of Scripture.

God blessed Job by restoring twofold all that Job had lost: twice the servants, twice the livestock and twice the possessions. Job didn't have twice as many children as before, he received the same number as before, but his older children were safe in the presence of their heavenly Father, so throughout eternity Job will enjoy the double blessing of family!

Job lived to see a part of His reward for trusting God, but he probably had no idea that His story would be told through the ages, that was a delayed reward, and for many of us we may have to wait until eternity to experience the full reward and understanding of our valley experience.

We may wish to turn back time and have God restore everything the way that it was before the valley, just as Job wished in chapter 29, but that doesn't usually happen. Usually, God works in us to increase our faith, our understanding of who He is so that He can be seen in a greater way through our lives! The reward for our faith may not be realized until we stand in heaven before Him and see the marvelous work that our faith wrought in other lives. I am sure that Job was amazed when he discovered that God planned to use his life to reveal God to all generations!

Know what you believe to be true about God and believe it.

Trust God.

Just between you and me, God: _____
_____
_____
_____
_____

The Blessing

Day 3

The Disciple's Life

When they observed the boldness of Peter and John and realized that they were uneducated and untrained men, they were amazed and knew that they had been with Jesus. Acts 4:13

We all know that the word "disciple" means to be a follower. If we are disciples of Jesus Christ, that means that we are followers of Him; we are to imitate his actions, attitudes, and words. When others see us, they should know that we are followers of Jesus.

When Jesus called out the 12 men that we have come to collectively call the disciples, they were ordinary, common men. They were men whom God saw not for who they were, but for who they would become. He saw hearts that were open to instruction and eyes and ears that were open for the long-awaited Messiah. He drew those men to Himself and began to teach them the truths of God.

During Jesus' three years of ministry with them, their understanding of whom He was increased.

Simon Peter made his great declaration in Matthew 16:16. **"Simon Peter answered, "You are the Messiah, the Son of the living God!"**

And again Peter demonstrated the disciples' belief and understanding with these words in John 6:68: **"Simon Peter answered, 'Lord, who will we go to? You have the words of eternal life.'"**

But in all of their time with Jesus, the disciples had a hard time understanding the disturbing events that Jesus told them would happen in Jerusalem.

From then on Jesus began to point out to His disciples that He must go to Jerusalem and suffer many things from the elders, chief priests, and scribes, be killed, and be raised the third day. ²²Then Peter took Him aside and began to rebuke Him, "Oh no, Lord! This will never happen to You!" ²³But He turned and told Peter, "Get behind Me, Satan! You are an offense to Me because you're not thinking about God's concerns, but man's." ²⁴Then Jesus said to His disciples, "If anyone wants to come with Me, he must deny himself, take up his cross, and follow Me." Matthew 16:21-24

The disciples had a partial understanding of who Jesus was. They understood that He was the Messiah sent by God, but they had not understood His purpose and how He would bring salvation to them; neither had they understood their own role yet as disciples.

Jesus had done all that He could do to prepare the disciples, warning them of the upcoming events, so that when they happened, the disciples would believe, as seen in John 14:28-29. After the crucifixion, we discover something else about the disciples.

Mark 16:11 _____

Mark 16:13 _____

Mark 16:14 _____

Luke 24:11 _____

The Valley of Glory – That Others May See Him in Me

John 20:24-25 _____

The disciples didn't really believe. They had believed the teaching of Jesus, but they had rejected his crucifixion. They had not expected their Messiah to die. This wasn't really the kind of Messiah for whom they had been waiting. They didn't understand a deliverer who would come as a servant, one who would come and lay down His life for others. They wanted a conquering hero who would deliver them from the oppressive Roman Empire. In the midst of their grief and confusion, they didn't even believe that Jesus had come back to life. They trembled in fear and hid behind locked doors, afraid for their own lives. They did not believe… until they saw Jesus face to face. When they saw Him, they believed. Jesus rebuked Thomas in John 20:9 for believing only after he saw and He said, **"Blessed are those who have not seen and yet have believed."** (NIV)

Jesus opened their minds to understand the Scriptures; He told the disciples that the Messiah had to suffer and rise from the dead and that repentance and forgiveness of sins could be preached in His name now to ALL men, and they were the witnesses of these things.

Jesus told the disciples in Luke 24:45-49 and Acts 1:1-8 that they would be the ones sharing this good news starting in Jerusalem, and He promised to send the gift of the Holy Spirit from the Father who would clothe them in power from on high.

When Jesus ascended into heaven, the disciples did not return to their hiding place behind closed doors; instead, they went to the temple in Jerusalem and, filled with such great joy, they praised God continually! Their fear was gone. The same risks that had frightened them before were still present. They again faced possible arrest and persecution. But the presence of the Lord had filled their hearts with joy and courage. They had indeed become disciples, believing Him and acting like Him in word and deed.

The disciples were willing to lay down their own pursuits and goals for the one great purpose of making Jesus known. When they endured persecution and trials and chose to respond as Jesus did, it made others uncomfortable. It is not natural to respond in this supernatural way.

Read Acts 4:1-22 which describes the actions of these transformed disciples.

What message were the disciples teaching in verse 3 that was disturbing the religious leaders? _____
_____
_____

The religious leaders didn't really want to hear a message about a man whom they had killed that had purportedly come back to life. That would have been uncomfortable. What question did the religious leaders ask the disciples? Acts 4:7 _____
_____
_____

What was the disciples' answer? Acts 4:10-12 _____
_____
_____

The Blessing

Their answer was powerful and convicting; the leaders saw the courage of Peter and John and realized that they were unschooled, ordinary men **who had been with Jesus!** You see, Jesus had given them the courage to face things that had frightened them before. Jesus' presence empowered them. They were called to be witnesses of all that they had seen and heard.

When the leaders of Jerusalem commanded the disciples to stop teaching and preaching in Jesus' name, how did they respond? Acts 4:20 _____

_____

_____

The disciples' lives had been changed. As they boldly preached the message that Jesus had come to forgive sins and give life, that He had suffered, died and rose the third day, thousands believed! Thousands became disciples. Thousands willingly laid down their dead, empty lives to embrace the life of God and allow Him to live through them.

Great persecution broke out in Jerusalem against all of these new followers of Jesus. As these believers faced imprisonment, death, and discrimination, they were scattered throughout Judea and Samaria. We may think this was an unkind act of God to allow such a thing to happen to these new followers of His, but what happened as a result of their great trial? Acts 8:4 _____

_____

_____

They took Jesus with them. In whatever experience they were, they brought Jesus! They preached the good news of Jesus with their words, and they verified their words with their lives. They imitated Jesus with their attitudes, their actions, and their words. As they were scattered, they were bringing Jesus everywhere!

I have heard that the entire known world was evangelized by the second century. This was accomplished by men and women who were true disciples. They allowed the life of Jesus to be lived through them. I have also heard the book of Acts described as "The Continuing Acts of Jesus Christ," because as disciples, we yield ourselves to the one from whom we are learning. Our lives yielded to Him will produce actions, attitudes, and words that are like Jesus'. Jesus lives through us in this broken, fallen world. We have the joy of sharing the good news of Jesus when we tell others about Him, and we have the privilege of showing the world what Jesus is like by how we live our lives. Together they become an unstoppable force!

Just between you and me, God: _____

_____

_____

_____

_____

_____

Day 4

They Gave It All

Therefore, brothers, by the mercies of God, I urge you to present your bodies as a living sacrifice, holy and pleasing to God; this is your spiritual worship. Romans 12:1

If you are like me at all, you grew up hearing stories about amazing heroes of the faith from Foxe's Book of Martyrs. The first chapter details accounts of the early martyrs of the church, including Stephen, from Acts seven, and the disciples. Each disciple is listed with the traditional accounts of how they met their deaths. Somehow when reading in the text of this non-biblical book, the words grip my heart with a holy terror. Maybe the detailed accounts stun me because I am not as familiar with the text in this book and have not grown familiar with the descriptions. Maybe the horror that grips my heart is there because I am reading accounts of people whom I have grown to love in scripture, and to hear so vividly how they met violent and horrifying deaths causes me to grieve as I picture the pain of their choice to follow Jesus; the choice they made even though it brought certain death.

The next chapters in Foxe's Book of Martyrs continue the bloody heritage of our church history and the individual stories of ordinary men and women who knew what they believed about Jesus and believed it with their lives. Their words, their actions, and their conduct reflected that of Jesus, and just as Jesus was not welcomed in this world, his disciples were not welcomed either.

I have begun to read through some of the accounts to refresh my memory as to some of the details of the personal accounts, and as I read, my stomach is churning, and I am crying. I am horrified at the cruelty and the torture these believers in Jesus endured. The final words of many of these faithful believers expressed their steadfast belief in Jesus. Holding on to their beliefs through the excruciating pain of torture, they chose to proclaim what they knew to be true about Jesus. They did not live to see their reward, but their faith was a sweet-smelling aroma to the Lord Jesus and He welcomed them safely home to heaven. With a kind and tender welcome, he wiped all their tears away and then showed them, I am sure, how their deaths made their lives a display of God's glory on this earth. He showed them how they were able to impact and change the lives of others by their willingness to die for what they knew to be true.

I have often wondered if I would choose Christ or if I would choose to save my life if I were in the same situation. The truth is that the answer is frighteningly close to me when I answer this simple question: "Do I die to myself daily? Do I choose Jesus over me on a daily basis?"

Again I want to weep as I think of all the times that I have chosen to honor the old man and the ways of the old man: anger, bitterness, slander, gossip, backbiting, gluttony, lying, greed, etc., etc. Every day when I am presented with the opportunity to live like a disciple of Jesus and display his glory to this broken world, and I refuse and instead wear the garment of my old man, I am refusing to die to myself so that Jesus can be seen in me. I have gotten off the altar of sacrifice and have chosen to love myself instead of loving God.

The Blessing

With the frequency with which I fail to honor Christ by dying to myself, I doubt that I would be willing to honor Him by physically dying. I pray that God would do the work in my life which would expand my understanding of Who He is and that my faith would grow to be so much more than words and conveniently lived truths.

I want to love God more than I love my life. Write out the following verses.

Galatians 2:20 _____
_____

Philippians 3:10 _____
_____

Revelation 12:11 _____
_____

We have been bought with a price, the precious blood of the lamb; we do not belong to ourselves. When we yielded our lives to Jesus Christ, we yielded ourselves to His will. His Spirit dwells within us to continue the work that Jesus began on earth: introducing sinful people to a Holy God who loves them and wants to forgive them. When He chooses to use us for this purpose, it is a privilege and while it may not be easy or pleasant when we choose the Spirit over the flesh, God meets with us and His glory is seen.

Just between you and me, God: _____
_____
_____
_____
_____

Day 5

For All the World to See

One of my heroes in the Bible is Paul. Paul was a man of passion and zeal. He knew what he believed, and his beliefs determined the course of his life. When Paul experienced Jesus on the road to Damascus, he experienced a life-changing event as his understanding of who Jesus was enlarged. His understanding grew and with that grew a faith that became steadfast and unmovable. His life became a pattern of stepping out in faith and seeing God work in his midst. Each time Paul acted in obedience with a step of faith and his faith was proven trustworthy, his faith grew and was strengthened to the point that he traveled the entire Mediterranean world proclaiming the good news of Jesus Christ, the Son of God, crucified, risen and coming again.

This message was offensive to the cultures and peoples of the day. They did not like to be confronted with the error of their ways. They did not like someone telling them that they needed to repent and have their sins forgiven. This angered some crowds of people, and it stirred the hearts of many others. The truth rubbed hardened hearts the wrong way, but it pierced and convicted the hearts that were seeking and tender toward the things of God.

Describe some of the experiences that Paul had during his lifetime of ministry for Jesus.

Acts 14:19 _____
_____
_____

II Corinthians 11:23-31 _____
_____
_____

I truly marvel that Paul's understanding of God was so absolute and real in his life that even when faced with the horrors of stoning, ridicule, rioting, imprisonment (in dungeons with shackles and rats and lice and rotten food), floggings with the cat of nine-tails, etc., Paul never lost faith. He didn't question why God would allow him to endure such trials in life. We don't see him curling up into a ball and refusing to trust God anymore. Each time that God moved in Paul's heart and gave him a burden to go and speak and share the good news, Paul obeyed. I think Paul had a wonderful charismatic personality. He was bold, yet he made friends with believers in all the towns that he visited, and he cared deeply about the growth of their faith. He wanted them all to know Jesus in the same way that he had experienced Jesus.

He never promised them that life would be easy or always good, but he assured them that Jesus loved them and that He would never leave them nor forsake them. He told them that Jesus would finish the work that He began in them. He described how they were all part of a body and how they all had specific jobs, and together, they supported and encouraged and built each other up when they obeyed God. He reminded them that an enemy was fighting for their souls and for the souls of their children, and they needed to be prepared and ready to do spiritual battle for their souls!

It isn't any different for us. This life that we live is about Jesus and making Him known; it isn't about our comfort and our pleasure and our pursuit of happiness and fun. Surely God does not withhold good things from us. He loves to see us enjoying life, but the danger for us is that in enjoying life, we lose our focus on our true purpose. Satisfaction breeds complacency. We get comfortable where we are, and we don't want to move away from that spot. We can become complainers and whiners, and we can actually begin to tune our ear to the voice of devil because he is actually saying what we want to hear.

God wants the people of this world, who are lost in the darkness of sin and in bondage to their old nature, to hear about the Creator God who loves them and has provided a way for them to experience abundant life. The kind of life that allows God to live through them in supernatural ways.

For Paul, he lived with an affliction that he had begged God to remove. God refused Paul's request and promised that His grace would be sufficient for Paul's need. Paul said that to live is Christ and that to die would be even better. His lived a life yielded to God, dying to self and telling the world about Jesus!

Another thought is that just beyond our human world, there is an angelic world that watches the marvelous works of God among the created, beloved race of Adam, and they wonder and worship.

It was revealed to them that they were not serving themselves, but you concerning things have now been announced to you through those who preached the gospel to you by the Holy Spirit sent from heaven. Angels desire to look into these things. I Peter 1:12

The Blessing

I have heard Ray Pritchard, the President of *Keep Believing Ministries,* preach on the idea that all the world is a stage for the heavenly beings. He was speaking from Ephesians 3:8-11. **"This grace was given to me—the least of all the saints!—to proclaim to the Gentiles the incalculable riches of the Messiah, ⁹and to shed light for all about the administration of the mystery hidden for ages in God who created all things. ¹⁰This is so that God's multi-faceted wisdom may now be made known through the church to the rulers and authorities in the heavens. ¹¹This is according to the purpose of the ages, which He made in the Messiah, Jesus our Lord."** He explained that the riches of Christ being distributed among the members of the body of Christ, His church, was a demonstration of God's manifold wisdom to the rulers and the authorities in the heavenly places. These heavenly beings could watch us live, and they could marvel at God's wisdom. Don't you love the idea that the trial you are in may be an opportunity for you to teach the angels something about God's wisdom and His character?

It is for the entire world to see—both the physical world of people who are either lost or dying apart from God and our fellow-believers, who could use the encouragement of our faith and also the spiritual world and the heavenly rulers—for <u>all</u> the world to see God's glory!

But I count my life of no value to myself, so that I may finish my course and the ministry I received from the Lord Jesus, to testify to the gospel of God's grace. Acts 20:24

Take a few minutes to quiet your heart before God; bring your present valley experience before Him and pray Psalm 84:5-7 to God.

"Dear God, You are the creator of this entire world, and You sustain it with Your sovereign will. Yet as big and as powerful as You are, You carefully formed man out of the dust of the earth, and You breathed into his nostrils the breath of life. You created the worlds, and You created us. I need to find my strength for this journey in You. I need You to uphold me with Your righteous right hand as I make this pilgrimage through life. You promise to strengthen me and to fill me with joy! Even as I walk through this valley of tears filled with shadows and pain, I do not need to fear because You are with me and You are my source of renewal and refreshment. The valley will be covered with the blessing of autumn rains. You will come and bring revival to my parched soul. I am strengthened by You, and I gain the courage to walk on, and then I meet You again and am strengthened once more; this is a pattern for my life until You come and take me home. Give me ears to hear Your voice in this desert place. I have been blessed."

Just between you and me, God: _____
_____
_____
_____
_____
_____
_____

Mountaintop or Valley – I Have Been Blessed

Our life stories are as varied and different as the people reading this. Some have suffered deeply, some not so much. Some have lived most of their lives on the mountaintop and others have lived in the valley, and many have lived a mixture of both. But when asked about our lives, we can give our entire testimony in four words, "I have been blessed." Without a doubt, our All-powerful, Creator God, who has promised to be with us and provide for us, the One who calls Himself our Father, the One who loves us, who is full of mercy, who is always good, and who is infinitely wise; He has blessed us. mountaintop or valley, He is completing a work in us which is for our benefit. He is in the transformation business and sometimes that includes the loving discipline of a Father. He is awaiting opportunities for us to trust Him and act in faith so He can reveal Himself to us in all-powerful ways. He has chosen some of us to be used as a vessel in which He can reveal His Glory to this broken and dark world. Yes, ladies, in whatever place we are in our journey of life, valley or mountaintop or somewhere in between, we have been blessed.

In I Samuel 7, we read an account of the Israelites getting their hearts right with God, and while they were all gathered together confessing their sins and worshipping God in the Valley of Mizpah, the Philistine army came out to attack them. The Israelites were terrified, but instead of letting fear cause them to doubt God or letting fear cause them to run, they chose instead to believe what they knew to be true about God and they asked Samuel to pray for God's hand to save them! Samuel prayed, and God supernaturally defended and protected them.

When the Philistines heard that the Israelites had gathered at Mizpah, their rulers marched up toward Israel. When the Israelites heard about it, they were afraid because of the Philistines. [8]The Israelites said to Samuel, "Don't stop crying out to the LORD our God for us, so that He will save us from the hand of the Philistines." [9]Then Samuel took a young lamb and offered it as a whole burnt offering to the LORD. He cried out to the LORD on behalf of Israel, and the LORD answered him. [10]Samuel was offering the burnt offering as the Philistines drew near to fight against Israel. The LORD thundered loudly against the Philistines that day and threw them into such confusion that they fled before Israel. [11]Then the men of Israel charged out of Mizpah and pursued the Philistines striking them down all the way to a place below Beth-car. I Samuel 7:7-11

Gathered together to worship God, the enemy attacked. Instead of running in fear or getting angry at God, they turned to God in unshakable faith, and God showed Himself strong on their behalf. The LORD thundered loudly against the enemy! I am sure that as the enemy got closer, the Israelites had not ever considered that God would thunder on their behalf. We cannot understand His ways, but we can trust Him.

Right after this supernatural intervention by God, Samuel took a stone and placed it as a reminder for the Israelites; he called it Ebenezer.

Afterwards, Samuel took a stone and set it upright between Mizpah and Shen. He named it Ebenezer, explaining, "The LORD has helped us to this point." I Samuel 7:12

Ladies, the LORD has helped us to this point! He has strengthened you for this day.

The Blessing

I think the most important lesson to remember from this entire study of scripture is that we need to know our God. We need to know what we believe about Him and then we need to believe it. We make choices based on that belief. **The people who know their God are strong and take action**, as seen in Daniel 11:32.

When we know God, and we know His voice, we can trust Him in the darkest of valleys. We have never been promised an understanding of why He directs our steps the way that He does, but this study has shown us that when our Father leads us through a valley, there is much to be gained. He doesn't allow us to suffer without it being for our benefit. When we yield to the work that He is accomplishing in and through us, His very presence becomes our source of strength, our springwater. His work of renewal and refreshment is like the autumn rains of blessings.

Let's turn to Luke 9 for some concluding thoughts on living on the mountaintop or in the valley.

About eight days after these words, He took along Peter, John, and James, and went up on the mountain to pray. ^{29}As He was praying, the appearance of His face changed, and His clothes became dazzling white. ^{30}Suddenly, two men were talking with Him—Moses and Elijah. ^{31}They appeared in glory and were speaking of His death, which He was about to accomplish in Jerusalem. ^{32}Peter and those with him were in a deep sleep, and when they became fully awake, they saw His glory and the two men who were standing with Him. ^{33}As the two men were departing from Him, Peter said to Jesus, "Master, it's good for us to be here! Let us make three tabernacles: one for You, one for Moses, and one for Elijah"—not knowing what he said. ^{34}While he was saying this, a cloud appeared and overshadowed them. They became afraid as they entered the cloud. ^{35}Then a voice came from the cloud, saying: This is My Son, the Chosen One; listen to Him! ^{36}After the voice had spoken, only Jesus was found. They kept silent, and in those days told no one what they had seen. Luke 9:28-36

If we were truthful, ladies, we would all want to say just what Peter did, "It is good for us to be here, let's build three houses and stay here!" Mountaintop experiences are amazing because we have such a clear view and understanding of life, our place in life and the direction we are going. We seem to breathe the fresh air on the mountaintop and feel energized and powerful. The disciples saw the glory of Jesus and their desire was, "Let's just stay here with Elijah, Moses, and Jesus!" The Bible states that when Peter said that, He didn't know what he was saying, and like him, we don't understand as much as we think we do when we are on those mountaintop places either.

Jesus and the three disciples came down off the mountaintop and experienced life in the valley.

The next day, when they came down from the mountain, a large crowd met Him. ^{38}Just then a man from the crowd cried out, "Teacher, I beg You to look at my son, because he's my only child. ^{39}Often a spirit seizes him; suddenly he shrieks, and it throws him into convulsions until he foams at the mouth; wounding him, it hardly ever leaves him. ^{40}I begged Your disciples to drive it out, but they couldn't." ^{41}Jesus replied, "You unbelieving and rebellious generation! How long will I be with you and put up with you? Bring your son here." ^{42}As the boy was still approaching, the demon knocked him down and threw him into severe convulsions. But Jesus rebuked the unclean spirit, cured the boy, and gave him back to his father. ^{43}And they were all astonished at the greatness of God. Luke 9:37-43

In the valley, there is brokenness, pain, and suffering. Here in the valley, there is an enemy whose desire is the destruction and domination of mankind. The disciples who had not gone up on the mountain with Jesus had been left to serve God in the valley. In Luke 9:1-2, the disciples had been given authority over all the demons, and they had the power to heal. **"Summoning the Twelve, He gave them power and authority over all the demons, and power to heal diseases. ²Then He sent them to proclaim the kingdom of God and to heal the sick."**

So what might have happened to these disciples who had stayed in the valley? What kept them from completing the work that God had given them the authority and power to do? I heard Pastor Ken Whitten, from Idlewild Baptist Church in Lutz, FL, preach on this passage. He pointed out the possibility that the disciples who had not been chosen to go up on the mountaintop top with Jesus were jealous of those who had been chosen for that experience. The evidence in Luke 9:46-48 shows that the disciples were concerned about which of them was the greatest. **"Then an argument started among them about who would be the greatest of them. ⁴⁷But Jesus, knowing the thoughts of their hearts, took a little child and had him stand next to Him. ⁴⁸He told them, 'Whoever welcomes this little child in My name welcomes Me. And whoever welcomes Me welcomes Him who sent Me. For whoever is least among you—this one is great.'"**

They argued about who was the greatest, but it says that Jesus knew their hearts. It may be for them as it is for us; sometimes we think that if we don't get to be on the mountaintop, then we must not be as loved or as necessary to God. Jesus, knowing their thoughts, reassured them that when we embrace our place of ministry, even if it's a valley ministering to a child, we are welcoming His presence in our lives and when we welcome Jesus, we are welcoming God too! This is how we become great: inviting God's presence with us, wherever we minister. There are no "greater" or "lesser" ministries with God, only faithful or unfaithful people.

In Luke 9:40-41, when the father of the boy approached Jesus, he said, **"I begged Your disciples to drive it out, but they couldn't." ⁴¹Jesus replied, "You unbelieving and rebellious generation! How long will I be with you and put up with you? Bring your son here."** Jesus may have actually been looking at the disciples when He said those words. It was the disciples who had been given the authority over demons and illnesses. They had been given a mission to go out and proclaim the Kingdom of God and heal the sick, and they were the ones who had failed to complete the directive that God had given them. If they had been pouting and jealous that they had not been chosen by Jesus to go up on the mountain, they were hindering the power of God that was available to them. In their choice to be jealous or hurt over another person's calling, they were powerless to complete the work of revealing God's power to people.

We may not like the valley places that we are called to serve. We may wish that we had been given a more comfortable, easier place to serve, but our call to service has always been to follow the example of Jesus Christ, and that means we take up our cross and follow Him.

Then He said to them all, "If anyone wants to come with Me, he must deny himself, take up his cross daily, and follow Me. ²⁴For whoever wants to save his life will lose it, but whoever loses his life because of Me will save it. ²⁵What is a man benefited if he gains the whole world, yet loses or forfeits himself? ²⁶For whoever is ashamed of Me and My words, the Son of Man will be ashamed of him when He comes in His glory and that of the Father and the holy angels." Luke 9:23-26

The Blessing

In one of the last encounters the disciples had with Jesus, in John 21:18-23, Peter was told by Jesus that one day he would die a martyr's death. When Peter heard this, his response was, "What about John?" Jesus told Peter that it wasn't any of his concern what happened to John, but that Peter should be faithful to follow where God called him.

We can be very much like Peter, not all that thrilled about the mission that God has assigned us. We can look at the valley places we are asked to walk, and we can grow angry, hurt and disillusioned if we look around like Peter did and say, "What about them?" Instead, we should view our valley as our place of ministry. Our assignment from God to accomplish a marvelous transforming work for benefit in our lives and in the lives of those around us. We will be strengthened in our walk through the valley, and as strange as it may sound, we can even experience joy in that valley place. We just need to hold on to the promises that we know to be true about God, believing them and acting on them. The disciples had forgotten Jesus' promise of authority and power against the enemy, and Jesus called them an unbelieving and rebellious generation.

When I hear prayer requests each week, I know that behind each request is a face. There is someone hurting, confused, in bondage, distressed, in agony or lonely. There is a soul in need of compassion and help. There is someone who needs to see Jesus. They may or may not know Jesus, but in their place of need they are desperate for Jesus to show up large in their lives, that their faith may be proven trustworthy and that their faith may grow in their valley place. Recognize when you hear these requests that God may have chosen you to be the vessel through which He chooses to reveal Himself to them.

Ladies, we cannot avoid the valley places. There will be many times in our lives when we are asked to walk in a valley of darkness that overshadows us; we cannot avoid it, nor should we ultimately desire to. The transforming work that God does in the lives of people is not usually accomplished on the mountaintops; it is done in the valley places. Accept God's gift of a valley assignment with joy, not because it is pleasant, but because it is accomplishing things of great value! Priceless people are being shown a holy God.

As we conclude this study on the valley, those dark times in our lives when things don't seem to make sense. When we experience the valleys that bring pain, sorrow and loss and it is hard to know which way to take, lift up your heads, reach out for the hand of the one whose voice you know, and follow the One who led you there. As we walk in faith believing God, His presence comforts us and strengthens us. Others will see God, and it will result in praise and glory at the revelation of Jesus Christ. Choose today to believe what you know to be true about God; hold tightly to these truths and let the Glory of God be seen in your life. Raise your Ebenezer—thus far the Lord has helped us, and we have been Blessed!

Happy are the people whose strength is in You, whose hearts are set on pilgrimage. ⁶As they pass through the Valley of Tears, they make it a source of springwater; even the autumn rain will cover it with blessings. ⁷They go from strength to strength; each appears before God in Zion. Psalm 84:5-7

www.ingramcontent.com/pod-product-compliance
Lightning Source LLC
Chambersburg PA
CBHW081348040426
42450CB00015B/3349